MW00413942

Black Lives, White Supremacy
and The American Fiction

Black Lives, White Supremacy and The American Fiction

Written in the aftermath of the shootings of Alton Sterling and Philando Castile and in clarification of the Trump Phenomenon

Brenda Wall, Ph.D.

For David

"It's okay. I'm right here with you."

*Four year old daughter's comfort of her
mother in the aftermath of witnessing Philando
Castile's shooting death.* [1]

Preface

This first draft of **Black Lives, White Supremacy and the American Fiction** was offered as a means of solution and healing. It was written in the first week after the killing of Alton Sterling and Philando Castile from the Dallas community, which witnessed both peace and tragedy in the killing of five Dallas law enforcement officers. While it is certain that healing can occur and authentic peace can ultimately prevail, the draft was finalized post Trump election and inauguration. With the dynamics of white supremacy becoming more overt and more widely recognized, it remains clear that its relationship to Black bodies remains woefully misunderstood.

Contents

Heartbreak

They did not know each other in life, but they became connected in death through a national mourning that once again forced America to address the question of deadly police shootings of African American men. Alton Sterling and Philando Castile were separated by state government and police department. Yet, both were shot by police multiple times with video documentation of their police encounters and their own brutal deaths--which television commentators reminded us "is disturbing" to watch.

Tuesday, July 5, 2016

In some ways viewing the shooting of thirty-seven year-old Alton Sterling in Baton Rouge, Louisiana was eerily familiar. He was outside the convenience store where he was known as the *CD Man* for selling CDs and DVDs. The store owner had known him for several years, and even bantered with him shortly before he was so shockingly killed.

Two police officers arrived on the scene in response to a call, apparently from a homeless man who reported that Sterling had a gun. Sterling did have a gun in his possession, reportedly for self-defense. Cell phone video shows Sterling being pulled over the hood of a car by one police officer and pinned down with another officer who quickly joined him in restraining Sterling before he was shot three times in his back and three times in his chest. The video was shared on social media that night, while the restraining officers both explained that their body cameras became dislodged. Blane Salamoni and Howie Lake, II were placed on paid administrative leave, which is standard police procedure, while the Department of Justice took the lead in the criminal investigation. As the story unfolded, we came to know Sterling as a man whose life mattered; he was a father, whose adolescent son was forced to grieve his father's death in the face of the national spotlight.

Wednesday, July 6, 2016

Another mother in another state said her son, Philando Castile, was "just Black in the wrong place.[1]" Castile was killed in a traffic stop in Falcon Heights, a suburb of St. Paul, Minnesota for having a busted brake light that wasn't busted.[3]

This time our hearts were broken as we witnessed the live streamed aftermath of the police shooting, which showed the dying Castile. His fiancée, Diamond Reynolds, live streamed the video on Facebook, which included Reynold's own detention and the innocent support of her four-year-old daughter, who was in the car during the killing. The precocious child can be heard saying: "It's okay. I'm right here with you." Reynolds also live streamed the agitated police officer on Facebook. Jeronimo Yanez can be seen pointing the gun at the dying Castile and defensively explaining his deadly action.[3]

In spite of the fact that Castile complied with Yanez's directions and did everything right according to police protocol, he was bleeding to death. Castile had a license for concealed carry, he had no police record and he was complying with police orders when he was fatally shot four times. First aid was not administered to Castile, even though the agitated Yanez did receive comfort and assistance.[4]

Thirty-two-year old Castile was also coming to be known to us as a man whose life mattered. He was beloved by the students at the Montessori school where he worked for ten years, and he also reared the precocious four-year-old encourager as his own daughter. This time, protestors initially guided the community's response. The governor, Mark Dayton, acknowledged the role of racism in Castile's death,[5] and President Obama offered condolences and a re-framing of police shootings of African American men to be an American problem.[6] However, the questions continued to surface, causing many to feel overwhelmed by a pattern of police violence that polarizes and intimidates. *What is causing this racial polarity and how can our African American community and nation be healed?* The answers are available, but sometimes can be as hard to embrace as the painful deaths we now witness on live stream videos.

It gets worse.

Thursday, July 7, 2016

On the following evening, as one of the nation's peaceful protests in Dallas, Texas was winding down, there was a sudden barrage of gunfire at 8:58 p.m. As the terrified crowd scattered, pandemonium ensued as shots continued. Initially, it was thought that two snipers utilizing high powered rifles from elevated positions were in separate parts of downtown in a premeditated ambush of Dallas police officers. Two active shooters were sought at multiple perimeters. Before midnight an identified person of interest turned himself in. At the same time another gunman, confined to a downtown building of El Centro College, was embroiled in police negotiations. This gunman threatened more mayhem hinting that bombs could be placed throughout downtown Dallas.[7]

There were other suspects taken into custody, including a female, and others who carried camouflage bags. One initial person of interest, Mark Hughes, turned himself in after being notified that his picture was being broadcast across television and social media. Hughes was proactive in removing his camouflage shirt and in surrendering his open carry rifle to police. He was eventually cleared and released following reported hostile interrogation.[8]

So much was happening: protestors were stranded in downtown and along with them, students at El Centro College and also personnel in the Bank of America building. All sheltered in place as law enforcement attempted to cordon off and secure the area. There was an incident of looting during the early uncertainty as to whether or not all of the suspects were in custody. Law enforcement was maintaining vigil at two hospitals, at officer homes and at the same time maintaining a large active crime scene in downtown Dallas.

But the worst nightmare for Dallas was not yet over. Twelve police officers were shot, five officers were killed, and two civilians were shot. Of the slain officers, four were Dallas police and the fifth was the first Dallas Area Rapid Transit (DART) officer ever to be killed in the line of duty. Shock and grief yielded to efforts to initiate appropriate narrative. *Was this domestic terrorism?*

It was a day of tragedy and terror but the early focus was on officer survival and honor. There was a human salute for two deceased police officers as their bodies were transported from the hospital. The first deceased officer to be identified was DART officer Brent Thompson. *How could such polarity exist in America today?*

Friday, July 8, 2016

The primary sniper was killed in the early morning hours inside an El Centro College building. At dawn's light, a twenty-block crime scene was established. All businesses within the demarcated area were closed, including Dallas County offices, El Centro College, and the Greyhound Bus Station. President Obama denounced the senseless murders as "vicious, calculated despicable attack on law enforcement."[9] Dallas Mayor Mike Rawlings and Dallas Police Chief David Brown held a morning press conference without sharing detailed information about the suspects in custody or the name of the killed gunman in order to further their investigation and maintain safety in the city. *We are hurting...we are heartbroken.*

Chief Brown described a robotic detonation,[10] which resulted in the death of the primary suspect. Before he died, the unnamed suspect expressed anger over recent police shootings. The delusional gunman said that he was upset about Black Lives Matter; he said he was upset with white people and with white police officers and that he wanted to kill them. He said that he was not affiliated with any group. The police chief added that the brave Dallas police officers put themselves in harm's way by running towards the gun fire in order to ensure that citizens would be safeguarded. *We don't feel much support most days.* The Dallas mayor encouraged prayer and support at a vigil at Thanksgiving Square for healing and unity at noon.[11] It was a statement of faith and confidence in the peacemakers in Dallas.

Joe Walsh, a former Republican Congressman from Illinois lost no time in using Twitter to call for a race war, a cornerstone of white supremacist ideology, with threats on President Obama and Black Lives Matter.[12] Later, he both retracted and denied the statement. Other inflammatory postings appeared on Twitter.

Later in the morning, there were heightened security concerns with a person of interest and a brief lockdown on Capitol Hill at the Visitor Center[13], another indicator of national distress. The country was hyper-stimulated around racial conflict. America was hurting and no one seemed to be clear on the way to heal. There was increasing confusion over how to separate toxic policing from unconditional police support.

Micah Xavier Johnson, a 25-year-old African American Army Reserve veteran who had served in Afghanistan, was identified later that morning as the lone shooter. There would be no mention of post-traumatic stress disorder as a possible contributing factor to his deadly act of violence until later news cycles.[14] The investigation would continue as chaos gave way to recovery and the nation's focus shifted to mourning and fears that law enforcement was under attack. It became more difficult to absorb the losses of heroic public servants and at the same time mourn the loss of innocent African American lives. Somehow, standing united with police seemed to usurp the readiness to stand united with justice across the racial divide.

Black Lives Matter released a statement condemning the violence against the slain police[15] even as they continued efforts to bring about a better world for all. Yet, the confusion over how to separate unconditional police support from confirmed police abuse was beginning to blur and shift the narrative. The polarity between police and the African American community was more readily identified than the capacity to effectively address the shocking violence that found outlet in both the devastating killings of police in Dallas as well as in the killing of innocent African American men slain at the hands of police with disproportional regularity.

It seemed easier to affirm heroic actions of slain police than to identify with the humanity of the African American men, who lost their lives without anyone bearing accountability or indictment for their deaths. The infrastructure for supporting police far exceeded the nation's call for honoring the humanity of African American lives. It seemed difficult to maintain support for police and at the same time support for Black lives. Instead, lines were drawn and both politicians and pundits alike spoke from predictable intransigent positions. Condolences were extended and explanations offered. Grieving families were burdened with the unrealistic expectation of providing solution both for their loss and for failed American domestic policies.

Peaceful protests would continue in Dallas, Baton Rouge, Atlanta, New Orleans, San Francisco, Phoenix and other cities mourning Black lives lost. Simultaneously, police across the nation were on high alert with concerns for copycat attacks on police officers. Regrettably, these fears would become manifest in more killing of innocent police and in more police shooting of unarmed African American men.

Saturday, July, 9, 2016

St. Paul, Minnesota saw more violent protests with an interstate highway being closed for five hours, yielding twenty-one police officers with non-serious injuries and one hundred and two arrests.[16] Heightened tension in Baton Rouge, Louisiana produced over one hundred arrests.[17] President Barack Obama spoke in Warsaw, Poland on the unfolding tragedy in Dallas, stating that he did not believe the United States to be "…as divided as some have suggested."[18] On the same day attorney Thomas Kelly, in responding to the shooting of Philando Castile, explained that "The shooting had nothing to do with race and everything to do with the presence of the gun that Mr. Castile had."[19] The narrative was shifting in a way that America could understand, but perhaps not with full awareness of implications.

Chapter 1
Establishing Context

November 24, 2014. *"Hands Up. Don't Shoot."*

We had been here before. On this date there was a return to national heartbreak and outrage. This date marked the culmination of a lengthy, well-orchestrated response to yet another police shooting of an unarmed African American male. There would be no indictment for the white police officer, who this time, killed an unarmed African American teenager.

This time the epicenter occurred in Ferguson, Missouri, a bedroom community near St. Louis, where two-thirds of the population are African American. It was a family community, although that has rarely been captured in the cascading media attention, which had galvanized the news headlines since the August 9, 2014 fatal police shooting.

Unarmed eighteen-year-old, Michael Brown was shot six times by white police officer, Darren Wilson of the Ferguson Police Department following a brief encounter and altercation. Brown's slain body was then left uncovered in the street for four and a half hours. From the very beginning, when twelve shots were fired at Brown, there were contradicting descriptions of what happened. Many witnesses stated that Brown's hands were raised in surrender when he was shot. Others explained that Brown was moving toward Wilson when he was killed.[1] This contrast in perception was predictably divided along racial lines and paralleled the racial tensions between the local community and their overwhelmingly white police department. Only three of the fifty-three officers in the local police department were black when the shooting occurred.

The neighborhood community would not remain silent this time in their response to the killing of Michael Brown and the aftermath that affected so many. Neighbors who actually saw what happened were incensed to see someone they knew so brutally shot, callously left in the street, and then maligned by an official reaction that initially appeared smug, calculated and indifferent.

The day after the shooting, the police introduced a scenario which focused on the physical altercation between Brown and the white officer who shot him, accusing the deceased Brown of assaulting the patrolman and reaching for the officer's gun. It would be six days before Officer Darren Wilson's name would be released to the public. The evening after the killing, hundreds of people marched to the Ferguson Police Department demanding answers in a peaceful demonstration.[2]

In North St. Louis County, however, looting, vandalism and rioting erupted resulting in thirty-two people arrested and two officers injured. The candle

2

light vigil for Brown had become chaotic with some
protesters looting neighborhood businesses on the live
and looped television news cycles.[3] Despite the
negative press, a community core continued to demand
justice with ongoing nightly protests and also with
what would become sustained, organized political
response. Within the week the police responded to this
pressure by releasing a surveillance video taken the
day of the teenager's death. A convenience store
robbery of a pack of cigarillos occurred ten minutes
before the fatal shooting and was quickly linked to
Michael Brown. Already the victim was being
portrayed as a criminal for robbery and for strong-
arming the clerk, who attempted to stop him. The
police narrative of justified use of deadly force had
begun.

The community narrative was also evolving. There
was protest, organization and demand for answers
early on. The protests appeared to be spontaneous and
peaceful, but also included volatile elements of rage
and resistance. Conflicting stories that initially fell
along racial lines illustrated the harsh contrast in
community and police perceptions.

Family of the deceased and residents of the
community laid flowers at the site where Michael
Brown's body lay on the day of the shooting. It was a
familiar custom of honoring the deceased. Reportedly,
a dog from the canine unit was allowed to urinate on
the memorial by an unidentified police officer.
Additional reports described police destroying candles

and flowers by driving over them, further inflaming the community.[4] By the day after the shooting, tension was perceptibly escalated, and local police stations prepared an unprecedented show of force to respond to demonstrators. In hindsight, the one hundred fifty officers with riot gear, police helicopters, rubber bullets and tear gas all only served to further escalate tensions.[5] The heavy militaristic response and aggressive readiness to control the community's reaction did demonstrate terrorism preparedness. *Who knew the terrorists for which the police department was so well equipped were the very citizens the police were sworn to serve and protect?*

The local police benefited from military surplus, which included military grade riot gear, armored vehicles and high-powered guns.[6] While this uprising became an opportunity to display their urban readiness, it may have inadvertently unmasked repressed attitudes. The numbers of citizens protesting grew substantially by the third day after the shooting. The refrain, *"Hands up. Don't shoot."* was echoed from Ferguson and quickly spread across the country. Community response became more focused, but also contained chaotic elements, which antagonized law enforcement. Provocation by police was recorded by national and international media, which spawned a third dimension of repression.

In addition to the shooting death of Michael Brown and the control reprisals that followed, Al Jazeera America issued a statement calling the Ferguson response an egregious assault on the freedom of the press.[7] First Amendment Rights were being challenged as both citizens and journalists documented hostile and abusive police interactions with of some officers of the law they encountered. The militarized police strategy appeared shockingly provocative and was repeatedly compared to war zone tactics. In fact, much of the equipment that was mobilized against citizens had been obtained through funding from the Department Homeland Security.[8]

St. Louis County Police Chief Jon Belmar defended his department's response to the civil unrest.[9] Governor Jay Nixon had declared a state of emergency at a press conference with curfew that was to be implemented starting at midnight.[10] There was nationwide criticism as images of excessive, repressive force resonated throughout social media. Amnesty International declared police actions such as aiming weapons at demonstrators to be human rights violations.[11] Several journalists were arrested, overcome by tear gas, and two reported being hit in the back with rubber bullets. Inflammatory moments were captured in which police threatened both protestors and journalists. Incidents in which protestors threw bricks, bottles and incendiary devices were also recorded. The peaceful demonstrations continued in Ferguson and across the country, as did strategy sessions that occurred away from the scrutiny of media.

This was the first wave of the community's voice. It was a voice that would not be silenced and would gradually become a mobilized network throughout the country. The price to be paid was high. More than a dozen businesses were burned, at least fourteen people were injured and at least sixty-one arrests were made in Ferguson. In spite of the scores of gunshots heard, some even heard on the nightly news, surprisingly, there were no fatalities. The higher price had already been paid in the senseless death of yet another Black man, which unleashed this response.

The funeral for Michael Brown was held two weeks later at Friendly Temple Missionary Baptist Church in St. Louis. Thousands from across the country attended the service, confirming the widespread support for both the family of Michael Brown and for renewed calls for justice. Mourners included the Rev. Al Sharpton; cinematographer, Spike Lee; clergy-activist, Dr. Frederick Haynes, III; Martin Luther King, III and three White House aides. This sustained the emphasis on social action and a call for law enforcement accountability.[12]

Perhaps, it was not anticipated that the fervent community demand for justice and police accountability would last for the one hundred and nine days it took for the grand jury to be impaneled, hear witnesses, generate the thousands of pages of documents in their secret process and make a decision for no indictment. Perhaps, it was the very lack of transparent process that would convince many in the local and national dialogue that the remnants of bias and racism stained all levels of this polarizing outcome. St. Louis County Prosecutor Robert McCulloch made the announcement of the grand jury's decision: there would be no charges brought against Officer Darren Wilson.[13] But while the police felt vindicated, the community of supporters for Michael Brown felt insult and outrage.

The prosecutor's statement appeared to substantiate perceptions of his enmeshed relationship with the police department. There was also concern that the delayed timing of the announcement was a thoughtless, if not decisive effort to exacerbate crowd agitation, because it was made after nightfall. The refusal by so many to accept the closed process and the pardon of deadly force re-opened the painful wounds of lingering racism and police brutality, especially towards African American men. Perhaps, it was surprising to many that this summer in this community, there would be a demand for justice, which rose from a dismissed and consistently undervalued community. But this community had repeatedly experienced disproportionate conflict, harassment and violent encounters with law enforcement, and they refused to continue their silence.

The question of what made Michael Brown symbolically ascend to level of national debate around justice was unclear. The timing was not assessed to be a determinant, nor was Michael Brown the poster child of innocence that so often seemed to be necessary as a prerequisite for respectability context, when fighting for justice policies. However, Michael Brown's life mattered.

He represented the invisible and nameless youth, who are familiar across marginalized communities. He lived in a world that regarded him as family, as emerging adult and as survivor. He was familiar to community and so was the process of discrediting his value and humanity. Not only did it appear to those who lived close to Michael Brown that his life was devalued and disrespected from the moment he was approached for walking in the street with his friend, but the defensive and indifferent posture of local institutions failed to strike a chord of fairness or respect. This disregard was apparent to the community in the twelve shots fired; the uncovered body being left in the street for four and a half hours and the prosecutor's culminating, theatrical defense of the grand jury process in its decision not to bring charges. In addition, perceptions from the violated community were routinely dismissed by a process that negated witness veracity and at the same time justified the blatant use of lethal force.

The Ferguson citizens recognized Michael Brown as the son of parents who loved him. They celebrated his accomplishments of high school graduation and his plans to attend college. He represented the many youth across the country who attend under-resourced high schools (his being in a district that had lost its state accreditation and was plagued with low revenue and low graduation rates). His life embodied the victory of

8

overcoming. His large stature was appreciated; it was not regarded as an intimidating threat. His position as an offensive tackle not only aided football advantage at school, but also lent itself as role model at home for being the "gentle giant."[14] He was funny and he was well loved by others. He was recognized for the way he dressed and he was affectionately known by his nick name, Mike-Mike. He was typical of many high school youth, who experimented with marijuana, but had no criminal record. On this day, he allegedly stole cigarillos at the local store. This micro moment of bravado would have deadly consequences. It would also amplify a voice that would declare that his life mattered; that Black lives matter.

Family and community insisted that Michael Brown's place in their lives was significant and of value. Law enforcement was equally as vocal in presenting the politically sacrosanct view of justice that all want to believe, even when it goes against statistics, life experience and an emerging challenge from social media. Camera and communication through social media would keep the Brown name and response before the nation.

In spite of the official grand jury response, Michael Brown's killing was surrounded by local witnesses, video recordings and scrutiny from national activist leadership that was invited early on by the Brown family. Not since Rodney King's video of March 3, 1991 did the community have such hard evidence of the violence, degradation and abuse that had been so

9

routinely downgraded and ignored by institutional policies. Depictions of justice that were framed by law enforcement were typically disconnected from the community it policed. The humanity of the community and the humanity of the criminalized were rarely recognized nor reflected in the media.

Law enforcement policies remained rigidly intact as men in the African American community were habitually criminalized and deprived of respect and due process. Hiding behind the distortions of black men as predator-criminal, law enforcement status quo could be increasingly excused, defended and disconnected from the marginalized communities they occupied. In the name of law, both apprehended criminals and innocents were too often mistreated through discriminatory policies resulting in unlawful outcomes of police brutality and death. This time, in Ferguson, Missouri, the community was weary of the politics of police immunity and took the opportunity to shift the emphasis from the abuse of law to a call for justice.

In the one hundred nine days leading up to the grand jury decision not to indict Darren Wilson, the voice of the community was unrelenting. On the day of the final verdict, Prosecutor Robert McCulloch was successful in reaching his desired outcome. A picture of insular law enforcement process, secrecy and legal vindication of police behavior resulted in establishment victory.

Yet, the establishment victory was problematic. The very disconnect from the demands of the community's call for justice would propel a movement that spread from Ferguson to the United Nations.[15] A shift in the nation's pursuit of justice was taking place. Community was in the process of reclaiming a voice that captured and strengthened a moral compass for fairness. While law enforcement continued to respond to the community with traditional practices of force and control, if not outright abuse and intolerance, these practices were beginning to be questioned with more rigor and sophistication. Utilization of social media was beginning to shift awareness in the broader community that law enforcement was sworn to protect and serve.

December 3, 2014. *"I can't breathe."*

Eric Garner died before Michael Brown. His death occurred on July 17, 2014 in Staten Island, New York, after he was approached by police for allegedly selling loose cigarettes. Garner had stopped a fight before the police were called, but he was targeted by the police when they arrived on the scene. When he denied having cigarettes and complained of being harassed, there was the move to arrest him. Video record shows that officer Daniel Pantaleo grabbed the much larger Garner from the back and placed him in a chokehold,[16] a technique banned by the New York Police Department.[17] Three other officers helped wrestle the large man to the ground and subdue him. Officer

Pantaleo further pushed Garner's head into the concrete, while four officers crowded over and around Garner.

This positioning interfered with his breathing. Garner can be heard stating eleven times, "I can't breathe" on video that went viral. They were his last words: "I can't breathe." The four paramedics who were on the scene did not appear to respond to the breathing emergency.[18] Garner was later pronounced dead at the hospital. The cause of death was determined to be neck compression and positional asphyxia, and his death was ruled a homicide. The four EMT's and paramedics were suspended without pay.

On December 3, 2014, the grand jury concluded its work and announced that Officer Pantaleo would not be indicted.[19] There would be no charges filed in the death of Eric Garner. A second wave of national protest erupted and this time the intensity was greater and more widespread.[20] Thousands of protestors across the country responded with outraged resistance to perceptions of police brutality, excessive force and a repeated pattern of non-indictments when men of color were victims. Police officers who killed African American men in situations that did not appear life endangering were systematically cleared by grand juries and never brought to trial. Perceptions that law enforcement was permitted to kill with impunity were increasing. Incidents of police abuse and exoneration were surfacing in the press, often in spite of hard evidence supporting the victim.

12

This time African Americans would march in cities from Ferguson to New York, across the nation and world, and this time there would be substantial support from a broader, more diverse community. Out of Ferguson and Staten Island came an impetus for change in national policies of police over surveillance and arbitrary intimidation and abuse. There was an intergenerational movement for change that started in Ferguson and quickly grew to include a diverse constituency in cities across the country. Communities could easily identify with the slain victims and often had local scenarios which echoed these same patterns of excessive force and unquestioned shootings. The exoneration of officers in the Brown and Gray cases served as both a tipping point for outrage in the African American community and as an anchor in mobilizing a larger community response to police abuse, racism and traditional law enforcement practices.

There were other police shootings that reflected the racial divide in police/community perceptions. Twelve-year-old Tamir Rice was fatally shot by a white police officer on November 22, 2014 for having a toy gun in less than two seconds after police arrived at a Cleveland, Ohio park.[21] The 911 call that the gun was "probably a fake" did not reach Officer Timothy Loehmann. The shooting was called in as a black male "maybe twenty." Whether he was twelve or twenty, he did not receive any first aid from the Cleveland police officers. Not until four minutes later did a federal agent, who was in the area, render assistance.

When the slain boy's fourteen-year-old sister ran to his aid, she was tackled, shackled and arrested, and placed in the back of the squad car of the same officer who killed her brother.[22] The children's mother would be threatened and maltreated as well when she arrived on the horrific scene. She witnessed her lifeless son's body and her handcuffed daughter in the back seat of a police car.[23] She was given the choice of helping her daughter or accompanying her wounded son in the ambulance. This callous treatment was incidental to efforts to control the narrative of the child's killing. Twelve-year-old Tamir Rice died the next day.

The pattern of presenting the victim as an intimidating threat was predictably presented, this time by the Cleveland Police Patrolman's Association president: "He's menacing." "He's a twelve-year-old in an adult body."[24] Predictably, after a protracted delay of over one year, the shooting was ruled justifiable. There would be no indictment.[25]

April 4, 2015

On the forty-seventh anniversary of the Martin Luther King, Jr. assassination, fifty-year-old Walter Scott was fatally shot in North Charleston, South Carolina following a morning traffic stop for a faulty brake light. Although Scott was stopped for a minor traffic violation, the encounter quickly escalated when the unarmed Scott, who appeared to be in routine conversation with Officer Michael Slager, bolted and ran. When he ran, Slager pursued and shot him five times in the back.

Initial police reports sounded exhaustingly familiar and happened to parallel the police report given for Michael Brown: the victim failed to comply with officer commands, there was a struggle and attempt to grab the officer's weapon, this time Slager's Taser. When a by-stander's video surfaced, it contradicted the evolving police report. Not only did it show Slager firing eight times, but it also showed him appearing to stage the crime scene later by re-positioning the stun gun. With this video evidence, Slager was immediately charged with first degree murder.[26] While this expedient action probably averted the community's rage towards an indifferent and scripted local response, the video also provided painfully graphic insight into police violence and police culture.

This scenario demonstrated almost universal patterns of insular and defensive police policies of self-protection, perhaps, to be in compliance with Supreme Court precedent regarding excessive force. *Graham v Connor (1989)*[27] determined *objective reasonableness* as a standard for assessing use of force in arresting law enforcement officers. Thus, predictable defensive claims emerge in checklist fashion documenting that the officer felt threatened, the unarmed victim reached for the officer's weapon, the officer feared for his life, culminating in the officer firing his weapon multiple times, which resulted in the victim's death. At the same time, a picture of the victim is produced which highlights past infractions and criminal history to reinforce threat, stereotype and marginalization.

The killing of Walter Scott re-ignited a national resistance to this nexus of racism and police abuse.[28] The racial disparity in arrests and police aggression towards African American men could not easily be ignored. This pattern served to illuminate national consciousness, while at the same time affirm what those living in marginalized communities have experienced all along. Black lives are viewed as expendable.

April 12, 2015

Twenty-five-year-old Freddie Gray was arrested in West Baltimore by a police officer after Gray made eye contact with him and started to run away. Gray was pursued and found to have a knife on him. He did not resist arrest, but video shows that he was struggling to walk as he was placed in a police van.[29] By the time he reached the police station after four intervening stops, he was unable to breathe or walk. His request for an inhaler was ignored. Medical attention was requested, but was not forthcoming. Gray sank into a coma and died a week later from spinal injuries-- injuries sustained while he was in police custody. His spinal cord was nearly severed and his larynx was crushed. No one could explain how, when or why.[30]

Six police officers were suspended as the official investigation proceeded.[31] Autopsy results were released at the end of the month,[32] indicating that Gray

died from catastrophic injury to his head when he
slammed into the back of the police transport van,
which apparently caused his broken neck. Gray was
handcuffed, shackled at his feet and was unrestrained
by seat belt. By the time the report was released to
prosecutors, there was also a spurious suggestion that
Gray's injuries may have been self-inflicted.[33] The
difference in this Baltimore occurrence of (at least)
police negligence was the context of documented
police abuse and unprovoked arrests in the Baltimore
African American community.

Even though there was an African American mayor
and an African American police commissioner in the
city, the pattern of police brutality was ingrained. The
city of Baltimore had paid $5.7 million in settlement
and another $5.8 million in legal fees to victims of
police brutality and civil rights cases since 2011 with
over one hundred successful claims. The details of the
cases were disturbing, egregious and included a victim
age range from adolescent to senior citizen.[34] That
history of brutality could not be divorced from the
frustration that erupted following Gray's death in
multiple race riots not seen since the extensive 1968
post-King assassination riots that consumed the city.

On the day of Gray's funeral, and incidentally on
the first day on the job for the nation's new African
American Attorney General Loretta Lynch, peaceful
protests morphed into chaos and riot. Defiant
protesters demanded answers and West Baltimore
rioting began. Fires blazed in the night; protesters

clashed with police; businesses were looted and the statistics reflected the damage to the community.[35] While city officials called for peace, youth called for answers, and disconnected national leaders positioned themselves to solidify the status quo.

Teenagers were characterized as thugs, even by the president and the mayor. There was blame from national leaders; the National Guard was deployed and curfew was declared in effort to restore calm.

At the onset of the turmoil, there were rumors of a "purge" that explained a heavy, militarized police presence.[36] However, these fears were unwarranted. At the same time, youth were getting out of school, many were stranded because there was no access to buses and trains as public transportation had been suspended. Buses carrying students were being unloaded and with the metro stations closed, the youth were stuck. Not gangs, not thugs, but stranded students who had no way to leave the area.

The police show of force and intimidation towards small groups of students fueled the very chaos they were preparing to stem. It did not work. The poorly planned efforts to prevent unrest contributed to the heightened tension and looting at the Mondawmin Mall in Northwest Baltimore and spread from there in Northwest Baltimore and to other locations in the city. By the night's end, Baltimore saw two hundred arrests, one hundred forty-four vehicle fires and fifteen structure fires. There were nineteen police injuries, but all were treated and released by the next day.

A short four days later, in an announcement that was startling for many, Freddie Gray's death was ruled a homicide and the six officers were charged, suspended from duty and taken into custody. Gray's arrest failed to establish probable cause and was ruled illegal. Mayor Stephanie Rawlings-Blake declared, "There will be justice for Mr. Gray, there will be justice for the family, and there will be justice for the city of Baltimore."[37] Yet, it was Maryland state's attorney for Baltimore City, Marilyn Mosby, who denounced the mistreatment of black men by the police in stunning remarks: "To the people of Baltimore and the demonstrators across America, I heard your call for 'no justice, no peace.' Your peace is sincerely needed as I work to deliver justice on behalf of this young man."[38]

Cheers came from protesters and predictably, protest came from the police union, which insisted that none of the six officers was responsible for Gray's death. Although the city of Baltimore agreed to a $6.4 million civil settlement to the family of Freddie Gray,[39] of the first four of the six police trials, there were three acquittals and one hung jury. None of the six would be found guilty of any crime.[40]

Chapter 2
Post Racial Society Becomes Racial

In the excitement and glee of electing a man of African descent to arguably the most powerful position on the planet, there was a rush to declare that the racial barriers had finally been broken. President Barack Hussein Obama was embraced as proof that the post racial society had come into fruition at last.[1] Yet, the backlash against President Obama had begun even before his oath of office could be taken on January 20, 2009. He would experience unprecedented, unrelenting obstruction throughout both his terms in office.

Perhaps because the U.S. had become so destabilized in the aftermath of the country's international response to the terrorist attacks of September 11, 2001 and the stunning domestic crisis which inundated the presidency of George W. Bush, there was distraction and easy dismissal of the junior senator from Illinois, when he began his run for president. However, Obama's new political machine was so unprecedented that effective counter strategy was not yet in place to defeat his exceptional fundraising, his innovative grassroots organization or his soaring oratory. He was among the first to mobilize those citizens who had been previously taken for granted. And he was at the vanguard when it came to utilizing technology and social media to organize his base, a base which included a burgeoning young and diverse electorate.[2]

With the support of those who had been ignored and thought to be irrelevant, Obama was able to move against condescending dismissal and the status quo until it was too late. He was the trailblazer for raising money and volunteers through the previously untapped medium of internet based technology and other social media.[3]

Obama was able to reach a significant percentage of those whose small dollars were historically underestimated, as seasoned politicians reached for major donors and public financing. His strategy yielded money, energy and electoral delegates. He won. This was a shocking reality for many establishment politicians, initially immobilizing them. Obama's victory served as a reality check, and illustrated their great disconnect from the changing American demographic, and simultaneously unleashed frantic efforts to recapture privilege and entitlement. Republicans and Democrats alike were shocked.

On the culminating inaugural weekend when Dr. Martin Luther King, Jr. would be celebrated in holiday for his transformative civil rights work with a national day of service, the inauguration of President Barack Hussein Obama would follow the next day and bring more than 1.8 million celebrants to the nation's capital[4] and to millions more viewing screens across the globe.

Two divergent trends began to develop. One was the declaration that America was now post-racial. There was seeming proof that was embodied in the highest office in the land. At the same time there was a reactive outrage and indignation that fueled immediate attempts to make Obama a one term president.[5]

This second trend yielded unprecedented micro-aggressions against the president and his family. There would also be tireless social and political pressure against Obama that crept into personal vendetta. Conservative radio airwaves, political pundits and frustrated citizens alike mounted continuous attacks on all that the president represented.[6] These efforts failed as Obama won a second term in office.

He ran against Governor Mitt Romney, a Mormon who represented the American values, which were often conveyed in code. Romney would propose putting America on a course to greatness with emphasis on job creation. (It would be Obama who would begin to fulfill this mission. By the end of his second term, unemployment would fall below 5%, a level not seen since the beginning of the recession of 2008.)[7] Romney was as self-assured of a win as Senator Hillary Clinton, Obama's opponent for the Democratic nomination, had been in 2008. Both underestimated Obama and the powerful organizational structure he created.

Obama's second term, however, did result in a continuation of the solid recovery of Republican control of the House of Representatives, which had

23

been regained in the previous mid-term elections. This resulted in their sustained resistance, which would bring the work and image of Congress to an all-time low.[8] It would be the strategy of the Republican Congress to shut down federal government if necessary, position new Tea Party candidates who were largely defined in terms of their vitriol towards the president, and to begin post-Reconstruction-like policies to block Obama's policies at the national level and retaliate at the local level. Voter suppression laws were introduced to eviscerate the protection of the Voting Rights Act of 1965 and to dilute the impact of those who had come to the polls for President Obama in a never before seen 69.5 million votes.[9, 10]

There were repeated futile attempts to undo the Patient Protection and Affordable Care Act, popularly known as Obamacare. This was the landmark legacy legislation of the president's first term and was repeatedly challenged (and defeated) at the Supreme Court level.[11] This attack was blasted across airwaves to galvanize those who were hostile to this new image of American leadership. All this occurred as American confidence in Congress eroded to lower and lower levels.[12]

Even with their unrelenting efforts to undermine his legislative initiatives, President Obama led the economic recovery for the country during the Great Recession of 2008[13] (Black America debatably excluded), saved Wall Street[14] and General Motors,[15] apprehended Osama bin Laden,[16] and brought home the troops from Iraq.[17] There was a lot going on. And through it all, the concept of post racial America stubbornly lingered. But little by little, this romanticized, post-racial perspective began to shift when the persistent pattern of police shootings of unarmed African American men (and women) began to saturate the news headlines.[18]

We were not post racial. In fact, the rage of white America would become increasingly obvious with troubling reminiscence of the past generation's racial unrest. Confusing and contradictory messages were being sent. While the fifty year anniversaries of the March on Washington of 1963, Freedom Summer of 1964, the Civil Rights Act of 1964, and the Voting Rights Act of 1965 were being commemorated during Obama's tenure, there were percolating voices of white rage that had not heard since the turbulent years of the sixties. While an ironic backlash was underway to reverse the hard won gains of the era, few initially recognized the startling degree of national polarization. Americans, angry at not having wage increases, disappointed at seeing jobs leave the country, confused at seeing the national demographic shift, frightened by the threat of ISIS, and defensively protecting the police with blind allegiance including the pardon of police brutality, constituted the disaffected.[19] And they all blamed President Obama.[20]

Barack Obama's occupying the Oval Office was symbolic justification for their rage and lost hope. Unidentified white supremacy was interwoven in this dynamic of despair. Many conscious African Americans understood this. And yet, when they named this dynamic, accusations of racism were vehemently turned and assailed against them. It all began to unravel when the pattern of police abuse was becoming more strikingly overt. It was racialized and it was increasingly being captured for posterity through video recording.

Could there be a connection between the African American man in the executive office and the unnamed African American men slain by police?

Black Lives Matter: It's in the American Script

Black lives matter and have always mattered in the United States of America. This statement is either obvious when interpreted at face value, or provocative when reflective of historic and contemporary indifference to black killings. The statement makes sense to all who see themselves as fair and who celebrate wholesome, American values. *All lives matter.* Americans have been immersed in a rhetorical American value system of "truth, justice and the American way."[21] It permeates our entertainment, our politics and our justice system. In fact, this familiar quote from the "Adventures of Superman" television show of the last century is an oft quoted phrase that capsulizes common American patriotism. In the TV show, it is spoken in a fictionalized context where there are no people of color. Superman-era heroes espouse the wonderful value system and related life

26

experiences of Clark Kent and Lois Lane. It is a symbolic fiction that comforts and inspires a nation rich in idealized, rhetorical justice. The popularity of the Superman characters and the enduring insignia remain familiar to both children and adults today. (In fact, Dallas Chief David Brown made reference to Superman when eulogizing slain Dallas police officers.[22])

In reality, however, the television series that captured imagination during the fifties created an entertainment where people of color were routinely absent in a normalized and accepted status quo. This offered a sharp contrast to actual American life and landscape.

Superman was popular during the same time the brutal reality of African American life was first being broadcast on national television. It was during the time of Emmett Till, Rosa Parks and the emergence of the civil rights movement. The images of lynching, and later attacking police dogs and water hoses turned on innocent African American citizens, stood in stark contradiction to the sanitized American script of "truth, justice and the American way."

It was the new medium of television journalism that supplanted the wholesome, uninspected image of American liberty and replaced this fiction with the stark contradiction of a hostile, unflinching, and dominating presence of American racism. The American fiction of justice was believable. But it was never fully true. It was carefully constructed and it had

27

tentacles of a long history that were rooted in the culture of white America. African American lives were an integral part of this ideal: their work determined the American economy.

Today, when "Black lives matter" is declared, the voice comes from a new, and previously unheard space. In order for the American fiction to prevail, the unexpected African American voice could never be fully articulated. In order for this fiction to ring true, Black lives needed to remain invisible and without voice. In this way, their roles could continue to be defined by the prevailing American fantasy. Rosa Parks was clearly not a part of this fantasy.

Invisible Man

Black lives mattered, but worked best for the American fiction and reality, when they were invisible, silent and controlled. This essential component of invisibility for Black lives has always meant that the national rhetoric could be constructed and maintained with little contradicting opposition. From the days of colonial America, young Americans were able to develop an idealized worldview, which was fresh in its democratic aspirations. (The play *Hamilton,* by Lin-Manuel Miranda, brilliantly depicts the struggle for power in the young republic and how self-interest determined the distribution of freedom.) This more perfect union was exciting with seemingly limitless possibilities of prosperity, power and land. The indigenous people, who inhabited the land would not

28

be invisible; instead they would be vilified, conquered and confined as obstructing the patriotic ideal.[23]

At the same time, the American values of "peace, justice and the American way," the values of God, country and apple pie, the values of "the blackest land and the whitest people"[24] could be preserved and strengthened through the authority of a newly written document. It would crystallize the beliefs of the young nation. The United States Constitution would be that hallowed document to guide across the generations and to be protected and defended with both enlightened and blind patriotism.

The enslaved African was important enough to be specifically referenced in this great document. He would be calculated in the equation for representation and taxation of his white owner. The enslaved African would be counted as three-fifths of a white person.[25] This Three-Fifths Compromise was enacted by the Constitutional Convention as a mechanism for distributing political power, and at the same time making it clear that the enslaved African was to be without political voice. Yet, it also indicated an aspect of the power and significance of Black lives. This compromise created a Southern power base that would retain influence and control until the Civil War.

The work that went into this compromise at both the Continental Congress and the Constitutional Convention demonstrated how both North and South had little interest in the humanity of the African, but tremendous interest in their African presence and in their astonishing profit margin. This is *how* Black lives mattered in America. It was an important statement on the failure of the founding fathers to recognize their dependency on the African and at the same time their failure to establish justice for him. Instead, the young country chose money over morality in an embarrassing failure to establish blessings of liberty for all.

This dependency on exploited African labor and the intoxicating profit which it generated would make the need for African silence and European denial even more crucial. It would prove to be a fundamental flaw in the framing of America, which would require cloak and distraction to cover this defective base. Christianity would prove to be fundamental to this process.[26] The true core of America would come to be clouded by the romanticized rhetoric of the Constitution and the professed righteousness of the Christian church. The heart of America would not be found in either source.

In order to sustain the economic vitality of the colonies and the independence of the young country, African labor would need to be guaranteed, controlled and managed.[27] The African life mattered as long as it retained profitability. There was no heart for African humanity, but there was always appreciation for the profit they assured. This absence of heart for the African was consistent with a confounding decision based on power, greed and insecurity. The evils of slavery would evolve into a carefully constructed institution which would permeate law, culture and

30

religion for generations to come. Economic and
political exploitation of a people was made possible by
legal sanction and compartmentalized morality. At
core for young America was not a heart for a more
perfect union, which was so eloquently delineated in
the revered Constitution. Likewise, there was no heart
for the justice and righteousness expressed in the
doctrine of the Christian church. The Christian
hermeneutic presented no apparent contradiction in the
teachings of Christ and the everyday life of whippings,
rape, forced labor and mutilation, which supported the
slave economy and white culture.[28]

Sunday school ideals of justice and compassion
were as distant from reality as Superman. Without a
deliberate or formal declaration, the heart of America
was not what it claimed was at heart. It was not the
Constitution or the liberty crystallized therein. It was
not Christianity or the love of Christ, both frequently
represented symbolically on national emblems. At core
of American culture was the protected and rigidly
emerging role of white supremacy.[29] Dominant white
power would prove to be the core value that insured
the profitability of slavery, that fueled the generational
hatred manifest in the Civil War, and which created an
apartheid system of injustice that would reach into the
future with little regard for its self-destructive
ramifications.

Deniability would become the spontaneous and
internalized response: *I am not a racist.* The accusation
of racism became insulting and offensive with no

regard for reality. White supremacy would become such an ingrained part of American culture that it would often become difficult to recognize. African lives would remain an important source of profit, and the vestige of white supremacy likewise meant that the African American would need to remain invisible, silent and controlled. White supremacy became insidiously enmeshed with patriotism and Christianity. And it would become even more complicated. White supremacy merged with white privilege.

White supremacy also became ingrained in its institutional form of preferential treatment and exclusionary legal and social practices based on racial identification. The profit margin shifted to an economy that included trappings of the slave economy: slave patrols, Black Codes, convict leasing, Jim Crow and in its most contemporary form, mass incarceration of African American men. Contemporary forms of exploitation also included profit from systems of substandard education, consumerism and underground economies of illicit drugs, human trafficking and illegal weapons. The pattern of silencing and blaming exploited voices by those in control continued to perpetuate wealth and fuel greed, which was legitimized across generations.

On a personal level, it was difficult to trace the detrimental impact of prejudice and overt racial abuse on white families. No questions were ever asked about the lingering vitriol of slavery and Jim Crow on white family relationships. It was there, but the link to alcoholism, domestic violence, sexual abuse and bullying was never considered in terms of unresolved generational entitlement.

Denial continued to be the primary coping mechanism for white America. Likewise, there were no questions asked about the national shift to criminalizing the African American as a means of maintaining subordination. In the name of the war on drugs, racial profiling or innocent fun, being Black was often sufficient cause for arrest. This practice was heightened at the same time there was a social shift to ban racial epithet in order to be politically correct. What this meant was that racialized incarceration could occur with tremendous devastation on not only the incarcerated individual, but also on the Black family and Black community. At the same time, self-approving white America would become mortified and often gasp upon hearing the word *nigger*. This denial was distraction from the epidemic numbers of African American men who were incarcerated with a justification reinforced through stereotypical media images, while white America could take pride in being appalled at the use of the *"N"* word.

From Nixon to Reagan to Clinton, the exponential arrests of Black men and the escalation of injustice economies had come to the point that America reached the highest incarceration rate on the planet with African American men comprising the catastrophic base.[30] This could not be possible without supporting law and law enforcement policy. While the criminalization of African American men is political in impact, it most often plays out with individual encounters between Black men and arresting police officers, who statistically speaking are most likely to be white men. These very officers are also seen on the evening news with compelling stories of heroism.

At the same time, racial progress appears to be taking place with misplaced attention on changing language by eliminating use of the *"N"* word.[31] Banning the word used by white family members, white fraternities, white beauty queens and white supremacists alike, created the illusion of post-racial progression, which disguises persistent, ingrained racism.

The devastating increase in criminalization of Black men has occurred against the backdrop of a patriotism which wasn't fully patriotic, and a Christianity which wasn't fully biblical. Both omitted the core teachings on justice, making it harder to recognize functional white supremacy. Those functionally supporting white supremacy most often do not recognize it in themselves and also fail to recognize the damage on their own personality and community. *Is it possible that there is an uninterrupted dynamic of white family dysfunction that is related to generational white supremacy?*

Contrary to slave myth and Jim Crow fears, the origin of domestic violence and sexual assault might be a lot closer to home. It would be too simplistic to explain that the one in four girls who is sexually assaulted before age eighteen[32, 33] can be entirely understood in terms of dynamics of white supremacy. However, unrecognized misogyny, mores of entitlement, hidden shame and unresolved sexual trauma complicate the discourse on cultural dysfunction in white families and community. White supremacy is toxic and costly across cultures.

Yet, in spite of the misunderstood personal and social cost of white privilege, it remains a dominant motivator. The rigid allegiance to white privilege often displaces principles of personal well-being or even principles of faith.

Adherence to the familiarity of white privilege often comes first and exceeds the readiness to do what is fair or ethical as long as it means that retention of white superiority can continue. Even where there is demonstrated damage to self and family, the white community rarely identifies unaddressed guilt, fear and shame in terms of dysfunction that is related to racism. There is higher emotional reinforcement for being white. Yet even here, Black lives do matter to the white supremacist.

The American fiction provides elusive economic hope and also an unquestioned Black scapegoat for conflicted, damaged identity. It would appear to those who are in denial that all lives matter. This statement serves to immediately neutralize the gravity of racialized injustice and the harsh reality for African Americans.[34] This disparity in perception and behavior originates in white America even when it is projected elsewhere.

The generalization that all lives matter as a counter to the declaration that Black lives matter occurs among those who are oblivious to their own participation in white supremacist values. They see through a lens that is culturally distorted. This distortion is magnified when the African voice is silenced. The distortion is further heightened when the Black voice that does speak is controlled and predictable, because it embodies the internalized values of white oppression and culture. The African voice that has been corrupted by a tainted value system that is compatible with white supremacy, is the solicited and typically preferred voice. Justice Clarence Thomas and more recently, Dr. Ben Carson, symbolize this to many African Americans. America has become so accustomed to the silent, invisible, controlled African American, that it is difficult for them to hear the unfamiliar, liberating voice of African humanity, authority and power.

Not until the self-empowered voice of the African Americans is more fully heard and their visibility recognized for its autonomous identity and world view will the racial conflict of America begin to be effectively addressed. Racism must be understood and addressed at its core. This means that white supremacy must be confronted in spite of the pain and fear it evokes.

What has been missing from the American analysis of racial conflict is the exploration of systemic white racism, what it means, and how it has damaged the psyche of white culture at both the individual and national levels. Racism is more comfortably explored with focus on the victim and isolated incidents of abuse. It is typically rationalized and occurs with a process of re-victimization. This misplaced focus permits re-victimization of children (and adults) in the name of diversity and racial pride. Even in February, there is a protected consideration of white America. *How many Black students are embarrassed through their re-victimization of slave association, stereotypical role models and criminalized images, especially in February?*

Yet, the value of the African life reaches far beyond the one dimensional embodiment of systemic racial injustice and abuse. While Black lives certainly reflect the presence of toxic racism and institutional greed, their liberated voice points to the impaired personality that perpetuates this pathology in American culture. Amazingly, or perhaps, strategically, the source of toxic, cultural pathology in the white community is never examined.

Chapter 3
American Racism and White Supremacy

The co-existence of European and African culture in America has rarely been analyzed in terms of how racism has damaged the racist psyche and the national community. Instead, guilt, fear, rage and projection have become hidden dynamics. African Americans have inadvertently rescued white America from facing its demons. During the non-violent movement of the civil rights era, many white Americans could begin to see themselves in reflections of abuse, hatred and ignorance that were uncomfortably close. Black America focused on the immediacy of dismantling segregation, not healing white America. Yet, many whites did begin the process of personal and community inventory when they stood with their African brothers and sisters to change the legal and moral climate of America in the late twentieth century. Many were selfless enough to pay with their lives for a freedom that remained elusive.

The Civil Rights Act of 1964 and the Voting Rights Act of 1965 birthed the hopeful but erroneous assumption that transformation of core racial dynamics had begun. It had not. While important progress was certainly made, core dynamics merely shifted and took new forms: police occupation of Black communities and the new Jim Crow of mass incarceration. A more honest and introspective work was needed to define these dynamics in the national context. Would there be perpetuation of discrimination, reconciliation, denial or retreat? African American activists were effective in modifying the law and changing social policy. However, what was missing was attention to the corrupting stain of racism on the white citizen.

Revisionist history over-emphasized the role of good white savior at the expense of truth.[1] Instead of the hard look at the evils of segregation and enslavement, the high cost to African American leadership and protest was minimized. There was the tendency to tell the story from the perspective of American fiction with the missing voice of African American correction, clarification, decoding and enlightenment. It was too hard to accept a different world view and too painful to take a full assessment of racism in families and in politics. The result was a perpetuation of denial. There was consistent retreat from addressing the core problem of white supremacy.

Historic Racism

Racism and its sister, white supremacy, have been historic problems since the country's beginning. They were problematic for President Thomas Jefferson when he wrote in his *Notes on the State of Virginia*[2] what he thought about the inferiority of the Africans including the ones he owned. It would take two centuries and the scientific breakthrough of DNA evidence to prove what everyone took for granted during the Jeffersonian era. Thomas Jefferson, who used his pseudoscience to promulgate the inferiority of the African in his ownership and also in those Africans who successfully liberated themselves in Haiti, was racist. For him, too, white supremacy was generational. His great, great, great grandfather Samuel Jeaffreson, who owned a sugar plantation in St. Kitts, West Indies[3] became wealthy from the labor of the enslaved. This racialized Jeffersonian privilege crystallized in Thomas, who was unable or unwilling to refrain from his exploitive sexual relationship with enslaved Sally Hemings.[4]

White supremacy often included a sexualized component which served as part terror tactic and part impulse gratification. That component can still be identified today. With President Jefferson, perhaps all felt the slate was wiped clean when upon his death, he freed the enslaved children he fathered with Hemings. However, he never recanted his destructive manifesto regarding African inferiority. Apparently, it was too hard for America to reconcile the common sexual coercion of a president with his slaves, when his writings were so eloquently supportive of their own white superiority. Denial was the accepted approach for two centuries. But denial worked.

From President George Washington[5] to Senator Strom Thurmond[6], America's attention has always been re-directed against prevailing sexually exploitive behavior of Europeans when it occurred in her leaders, as long as it co-occurred with white supremacist rhetoric and policies. Those Africans who were abused, knew the reality, but their voices were nullified. They did not count. Desperate efforts to blame the victim of lasciviousness was a safe and convincing hiding place for white fear and sexual immorality, as long as there was power to maintain the fiction.

The myth remains as clouded and confusing for us today, especially where the lens that perpetuates such a bifocal distortion remains unchallenged. The power broker would be excused (e.g. Strom Thurmond, the Klan rapist or the fraternity brother) if he were hidden behind the language, symbols and legal sanction of racialized denouncement and hatred. This duality of morality has been permitted since the founding of this country, because of the tremendous wealth generated and the moral freebie of no accountability, as long as the egregious behavior occurred with disempowered, marginalized others.

The continuity of violence against African American others and sexual preoccupation with African American others has been met with projection and with blame imposed on the innocent. From captivity and enslavement to modern abuses against Black men, scenarios have effectively projected the blame onto the African American victim. White America can more readily negotiate the source of the problem when externalized and placed on African Americans, which provides space for white America to

42

remain unquestioned, virtuous and non-accountable. Where there is interracial violence, the source of the problem has been pre-determined to be the African. When there has been even the threat of sexual exploitation, the problem has been declared and *proven* to lie with the African.

Projection of the negative began with the earliest rape of African women and boys against the counter narrative of white women being portrayed as the innocent object of African desire. That deliberate deception provided justification for lynching, rage and mutilation. Yet, white access to the disparaged victim and community has been consistently maintained. There has always been an overt effort to distance the African, but always with uninterrupted sexual access. That pattern of behaving egregiously while loudly proclaiming innocence can still be seen today. As long as there is a following which is also willing to ignore fact and reality, emotions and economics outweigh justice.

Whether slave quarters or ghetto, the African American was always kept near. With so much chaos and pain, there was rare attention to understanding those instigating and perpetuating the violence. Even with evidence of widespread maltreatment, the impact on white personality and culture was uninspected as long as propaganda of American values remained in place to disguise pathological behavior. Criminal behavior among white Americans became legally sanctioned and pardoned.[7] This created a divergence in legal behavior and authentic justice.

It was legal to own, hunt, whip, maim and take the lives of slaves. Legal sanction became increasingly repressive in order to maintain control of growing numbers of enslaved Africans. Repression was manifest in both common practice and legal sanction.[8] It was eventually determined by the Supreme Court that no person of African descent could be or was ever meant to be citizen of the United States of America.

In the Dred Scott decision of 1857, law preempted justice.[9] The Black man had "no rights which the white man was bound to respect."[10] Ramifications of this argument would be seen in the Plessy v. Ferguson decision of 1896,[11] which gave constitutional support for state laws that embraced segregation. Jim Crow was legal. It would remain legal until 1954 and it would remain custom even after that.[12]

It is important to note, that the African presence always meant white access to Black lives, but only to controlled Black lives. They could be on the bus, but only in the back seats. Degradation was a component of the cultural control, which reinforced legal control. This intimate relationship provided for both sexual and violent outlet, but with legal and cultural protection for the perpetrator.

In 1954, the *Brown v Board of Education*[13] decision determined that state laws supporting segregated public education were unconstitutional. When legal sanctions shifted, there was more reliance on cultural controls. White supremacy would have to be maintained through volatile practices of intimidation, abuse and economic control. Coded language and symbols would indicate both danger for African Americans and pride for their oppressors. The Confederate battle flag made its re-appearance among those supporting segregation with the Dixiecrat Party[14] in 1948. Although the Army of Northern Virginia battle flag[15] never historically represented the Confederacy, it did come to represent both southern white arrogance and protest against desegregation.

Even after 1954, law was still used to maintain white supremacy through judges and juries who remained loyal to their supremacist world view. The anger and hatred lingered and found institutional outlet for those still in authority. Impunity was extended through the court system and through laws which disproportionately impacted marginalized communities. The history of slave controls morphed into law enforcement practices that permitted occupation of Black communities. These communities were separated, but always accessible. Although law enforcement became more nuanced, the remnants of the past remained entrenched in the law and also in the policing of America. The law and the enforcement of the law were extensions of a long history of white supremacy and white control. The psycho-political rigidity of white control would find its place in current denial and debate. Because there was avoidance of what this looks like in a national context, healing and

45

resolution remained painful, protracted and weak. There was insufficient attention to the white perpetrator and their dominant system of institutional control.

Heart of America

What has always been more important than God or country in America has been white privilege. The Ku Klux Klan[16], which came into being as a direct response to the gains of emancipation and reconstruction, used terror as a means of restoring white supremacy. With conspicuous, terrorizing symbols of the flag and the cross, there would be retaliation and the utilization of the tools of enslavement to maintain power. Layers of protection were in place with law, with law enforcement, with culture and with unexamined social practice. Clearly, not all southerners were Klan members, but Klan control did permeate culture and political office.

With a political bargain in the form of the Compromise of 1877,[17] Republican Rutherford B. Hayes got the White House in exchange for withdrawal of U.S. troop protection for African American bodies in the South. This permitted disenfranchisement for African Americans and accelerated a return to slave-like conditions. White supremacy was reflected in the nation's decision to retreat from a moral responsibility in the same way its founding fathers did.

Since there was no legal repercussion, criminal character evolved in the white supremacist alongside patriotism. The two, in fact, became intertwined. This made it difficult to differentiate criminal practice from idealized values. People who raped, killed and abused professed belief in the values of God and country. The purity that was held up for public consumption became hard to separate from the reality of illegal and immoral behavior.[18] The soul of America was eroded and the only ones who noticed were those who were invisible to the American fiction.

That was Then

Slavery no longer legally exists (unless there is a careful reading of the Thirteenth Amendment to the United State Constitution).[19] In fact, Jim Crow no longer technically exists.[20] Thus, it seems pointless, uncomfortable, and unnecessary for Americans to recall the horrors of their turbulent racial past. African Americans are accused of dwelling on the past instead of moving on, while white Americans defensively explain their current disconnect from slavery, reminding all that they are not slave owners and they are not racists.

Although white America may feel functionally disconnected from the slavery of the past, symbols of the Confederacy were resurrected during the Superman years.[21] There was an invigorated battle cry to resist Jim Crow and forced integration with ubiquitous Confederate symbols on flags, mascots and clothing, often alongside the American flag. Reconciliation was never a goal and was not meant to provide closure during Reconstruction, during the Civil Rights period or during the post-Obama years.

Instead there would be continued disavowal and denial. White supremacy continued to serve as a birthright and provide continuity with the idealized American fiction. It was strategically necessary to have a more extreme expression of white supremacy in order to offset mainstream politics.[22] The Klan sheets on Saturday could be safely condemned, while their disrobed presence on Monday went unquestioned in local government representation.

White America has failed to recognize how its history with slavery has had an impact on its current values and behavior.[23, 24] It is burdensome discussion, especially in post racial circles. Politics and confused racial identity further complicate the matter. For the unresolved white person and even for the *good* white American, there has been failure to examine how white supremacy functionally operates. White supremacy goes far beyond politics.[25] It is a safe haven, which is immune from inspection and is rationalized by those with less extreme expressions.

The generational entrenchment of white nationalism in America presents another major dynamic. White privilege and entitlement are evident in both institutional structures and also in dormant values[26] that were last openly expressed during the civil rights conflict. Those white Americans who spat, cursed and assaulted during the Superman years, have largely aged out of public leadership roles. Yet, remnants of their belief system are evident in institutional constructs including corporate wealth, police associations, and voter suppression. Their intact beliefs are communicated through their progeny in school curriculum, behavioral bullying, efforts at political correctness and wealth disparity.

Discomfort or resistant anger surfaces when African Americans become visible and deliberately choose to challenge the American continuum of denial, distortion, and rationalization. As obvious as it may be, contemporary racism is ignored as a factor in the interpersonal and cultural American experience. The demographic has shifted, though, and in younger Americans, where there is less awareness of history, there is often greater tolerance.[27] Yet, this does not eradicate current influences of hostile or permissive discrimination. Regrettably, this ignorance leads to American self-delusion.

The wealth that has been generated from black bodies remains multi-layered, but poorly understood. Whether incarceration[28] or sub-prime mortgage exploitation[29], the profit margin from oppression remains lucrative. From the wealth that has been generated from illicit drug trafficking to the economy that is built around the highest incarceration rate in the world, the invisible continue to create prosperity for those who manage the American script.[30] The economic and legal sanctions provide reward and

49

protection for those in power, while permissive discrimination is achieved through a passive acceptance, uncritical analysis and manipulation of the rhetoric.

White supremacy is not experienced as white supremacy by those who maintain the American fiction. It seems normal.[31] It is experienced as adherence to a Constitution that too few are educated to understand; as state's rights which can be a comfortable argument for maintaining a divided society, and as God's love for America. The work of the civil rights era unmasked the ugliness of white supremacy, and in so doing demonstrated an aspect of America's heart. White supremacy could not understand itself nor its contradictions in idealized belief and insular behavior. White police, white families and white individuals have been so removed from the Black community that the Black voice of authority and self-correction is problematic.

The lynching that defined the era leading up to the civil rights struggle now reappears in the form of criminalization and vilification of black men that pardons the perpetrator for killing and then blames the victim for being killed. The spectacle of the lynched black body was meant to terrify a community and perpetuate prevailing white power and white privilege.[32, 33] The uncovered body of Michael Brown for four and a half hours was reminiscent of the same insult and offense for the black community. The community had had enough and there was a multi-

50

tiered response. From riot to organization, from veterans of the civil rights movement to millennial resistance, from the local resident to the national activist, the attention of the country and world would again focus on the degree of danger faced by African American men and women.

The heinous death of Emmett Till resulted in the unstoppable energy of the civil rights movement. It was also a death in which the killers were found not guilty. They were acquitted in 1955. Even though the murderers admitted to killing Till, double jeopardy prevented them from being re-tried.[34] However, a shift in culture followed: freedoms were demanded because of mass refusal to accept the blatant disregard of African American life. This time the deaths of Michael Brown, Philando Castile, and so many others ignited demonstration, debate and opportunity to recover to a higher level of justice and understanding. Black lives, the protesters proclaimed, have human value.

Chapter 4
Black Lives Matter

The dismissed African American lives were never oblivious to the process of oppression. How could they be? They were a culture of survivors with fierce determination to flourish at both the family level and community level. Yet, the capacity to see humanity across the racial and economic divide was not easy for African Americans either.

Some remained true to an identity and world view reflective of their truth and strength. Others found it easier to cope by internalizing the values of the ubiquitous white presence. There was another group with a blended coping style which incorporated a dissonant identity from both spheres. However, often without realizing it, both races have been conditioned to value some people and to devalue and distance others. This personal ethnocentrism has caused many to insist that personal and community world view is the same for all. It is not.

It is, for example, hard for many to see the source of the racialization of criminals that has taken place in America. The war on drugs has shifted to a war on African American youth and men.[1,2] complicating perceptions of African American men. The very strategic racialization of criminals, who are portrayed regularly on the daily news cycles as impoverished predators and criminals, effectively condition perceptions. At the same time, new American fiction is being generated. The scores of innocent African American men who have been killed by white police officers have been camouflaged by the conditioning of America.

It seems to make sense, when conflict is viewed through the lens of functional oppression. It permits racism to be addressed at a superficial, but predictable emotional level. Racial conflict is met with venting, apathy, defensive accusation and increased agitation-- on both sides of the racial divide. It becomes too painful and overwhelming to acknowledge the differential impact of racism, because it feels too large, too ingrained and too hopeless to address. Thus, it is misrepresented as an isolated occurrence and minimized in the face of the same reality which has been evident since enslaving America of 1619. Instead of clarifying dynamics, dialogue changes almost immediately to denials, blame and emotional denouncement.[3]

There is typically an immediate retreat from productive discussion with self-reassuring denial, artificial claims that balance exists and failure to recognize how history impacts fear. This approach reinforces and sustains the problem as well as securing the wealth at hand. It is easier to justify policies, retain focus on criminalization and pretend that racial dynamics are irrelevant. It does not matter that

54

America is not post racial. White supremacy works as long as it is verbally denounced. The regard for African American bodies remains conditioned by images of criminalization, history of Jim Crow and slavery and also the dangerous assumption that racism is historical and not contemporary.[4]

In spite of this, there now emerges nationwide re-direction in law enforcement to challenge policies on grand jury/prosecutor bias, as well as introduction of police de-escalating techniques, anti-bias training and use of body cameras. Even in the midst of this shift, the core problem of white privilege is ignored. Interesting that challenge to this injustice does not flow from the presidential level, but again is generated from grass roots leadership. There must be a shift in the narrative not only to challenge injustice, but also to address the divisive remnants of racism that morph into deadly policies and immobilize citizens with apathy, guilt, fear and rage on both sides of the racial divide.

Re-centering

The death of Michael Brown illuminated a reality that many African Americans experience regularly. Even African American police officers understand that there can be a difference in routine traffic stops when they are not in uniform. Just as establishment America finds it difficult to recognize the magnitude of prevailing injustice, so do many African American victims, who actually live in occupied communities. Their efforts to obtain legal redress typically end with little success, causing many families to feel isolated, powerless and disenfranchised. African American men continue to be criminalized and seen through a lens that negates their worth to society. This criminalization makes it easier to dismiss their value and then condemn them when they are killed. The process of character assassination reinforces stereotypes[5] and makes it easier for law enforcement to perpetuate unfair policies. While these policies serve to destabilize local communities, at the same time they can operate to demoralize and frustrate many in the larger community.

As a means of coping, African Americans sometimes accept the negative conditioning and ascribe to the identity imposed by white dominance.[6] Debilitating internalization of oppression coupled with external controls continue to burden African American family and community, while resulting in hidden gains for those manipulating the script. In addition to living in occupied communities stifled with silenced voices, marginalized masses and dismissed bodies, there is a duality of survival. There can be both a belief in the false narrative as well as a counter defiance of insight and untapped power among those in the community. The stereotype dominates the public script and often complicates coping at the community level, but it does not result in blanket silence nor does it negate the resilient love, survival and resistance common to African American community.

White America has a related challenge. With white supremacy and white privilege denied to the point of being exempt from critique,[7] white America has become insensitive to its moral bankruptcy. With Christianity in the forefront, unexamined positions result in the misguided conclusion that America and its institutions are sound and virtuous. The lessons of Dr. Martin Luther King, Jr. may have produced meaningful changes in law and society, but policies of white privilege have grown with minimal opposition. For example, Southern Baptists[8] and the United States Congress,[9] have both apologized for slavery (almost a century and a half later), but with no corresponding shift in their structure or function. In fact, Congress issued their apology with the stipulation that it not be considered the gateway for reparations.[10]

It is difficult for white Americans to struggle with white supremacy. The outcome is often one of self-congratulation rather than meaningful impact. It is dangerously counter-productive, because policies of abuse remain unaddressed.

When the police are involved in shooting unarmed African American men, there is often more continuity with the policies of past policing than with community protection and justice. The images and language have persisted from the slave catcher to modern police protocol. Yet, few realize the law enforcement connection with the Black Codes[11] of post-Reconstruction. These newly created laws served to maintain control of the labor of the freed community

57

after Emancipation by incarcerating the formerly enslaved for minor infractions and committing them to involuntary labor. Those restrictions and control of black labor were directly related to white retribution, white wealth and white power. Initially there was no need to criminalize, because black labor was experienced as an entitlement in the aftermath of slavery, and when cheap labor was needed.

Today the parallels remain; they can be seen in the form of the epidemic incarceration rate of African American men and in the continuity of disparate wealth distribution. This creates a felony class with few civil rights and a privileged class that benefits materially from failed drug policies for the powerless, combined with protective policing policies for the powerful.[12] The policies of institutional racism have never been broadly studied or understood with the goal of eliminating them, because they serve such a beneficial outcome for the status quo.

The average white American or white police officer would not be able to recognize the straight line continuum from legalized slavery to the legalized arrest rates in the African American community. They would also be unable to trace the economies generated. The role of the police in the African American community is not to protect and serve even where there are good officers or dedicated Black police chiefs. There are many wonderful police. However, service and protection are not the same across marginalized and mainstream communities.[13]

58

The purpose of African American community policing is defined by that first line of community interface which results in that disproportionate number of bodies fueling high incarceration. It is not possible to have one out of three African American men registered in the criminal justice pipe line without vigorous, sustained policing. The policing begins in public schools, is solidified through the court system and results in an unconscionable rate of incarceration.[14] The occupied community recognizes this process of control. The system of abuse and police killings yields a social problem as well-defended as slavery. The big difference is the degree of visibility. The outcome is evident in racial disparity, but the process of white dominance has remained covert and safely obscured. That means it is rarely addressed.

Resurgence

In post racial America, there was an immediate racialized response to Obama's presidency with full-throated, political resistance.[15] There were some catastrophically deep feelings. The Tea Party[16] came into being, largely defined by its anti-Obama agenda. Eventually the public framing shifted to more general conservative values of reduction in government spending and lower taxation. At the same time, there was also much coded language, expressed by indignant and frustrated conservatives. The national dialogue evolved in terms of both personalities and policies, which emboldened those Americans vested in the American fiction.

From Romney's *Believe in America*[17] to Donald Trump's *Make America Great Again*[18], there was appeal to the electorate with a claim that jobs creation would be central (a minimized Obama accomplishment[19]). These Republican presidential candidates appealed to the segment of America that admired their personal wealth and accepted their innuendo of white pride. Support for the American fiction was reflected in their statements. Presidential Republican candidate Romney dismissed 47% of American voters he viewed as "dependent on the government" and "who believe they are victims." Presidential Republican candidate Donald Trump heavily utilized insults to defiantly malign Mexicans, Muslims, women and many others. His immigration policy of deporting all undocumented Mexicans and building a wall on the Mexican border, which the Mexican government would be forced to finance, became an early rallying cry for his constituents. While Trump initially refused to disavow the support of the Ku Klux Klan for his candidacy, he eventually denied that he is a racist person, stating that he does *"not have a racist bone in my body."*

What is interesting is not that Donald Trump may be a racist or even that he is identified as racist by many in the country. What is both interesting and troubling is that so many in white America, whether they support him or ridicule him, are unsure of how to evaluate his positions on race relations, which have clear dynamics of xenophobia, misogyny and white privilege. Discussion of the core appeal of racism was initially avoided or minimized. Instead components of racism were addressed separately: anger, economic insecurity, fear and scapegoating. The readiness of white America to deny the presence of white supremacy and racism ensures that confusion and limited understanding can persist.

I am not a racist. Presidents George Washington, Thomas Jefferson and Andrew Jackson, for example, were not viewed as racists either. They were seen as patriots who merely followed the law and the mores of their time. This disclaimer is consistent with the pattern of supremacist behavior today. And it occurs among police, among presidential candidates and of course, more extremely in overt, hate groups.

Racism and white supremacy have become the tools of maintaining the balance of wealth in American society and also the values of the culture that protect this system. Although we are no longer an agrarian society, slave labor remains crucial, however its form has shifted over time.

Reconstruction was abandoned in order that the North could focus on its growing industrialization and the South be permitted to regain a semblance of economic recovery. North and South reconciled. The newly emancipated were left defenseless to face punitive retribution for war and a return to violence, sexual exploitation and degradation all with no repercussions for the offender. Forced labor through peonage,[20] stripped voting rights,[21] and controlled labor through sharecropping[22] helped maintain the power advantage of the South and the new script. Revisionist history replaced the cruelty of chattel slavery with tales of a loving master and subordinate, thankful class of labor.[23] Those who were not thankful were portrayed in negative terms that would justify the wanton abuse they received. They were seen as brutish, predatory and threatening in order that there be no reprisal or guilt for repressive acts of retaliation. (Freud might call this projection.) Black men were depicted in culture as dangerous sexual predators, while white supremacists maintained their practice of control through intermittent sexual violence against children and women.[24] White supremacy rarely rose to a conscious, articulated reality as long as the invisible could remain controlled and silenced and the American fiction could be perpetuated.

The control over the formerly enslaved was maintained through terrorism, a forced caste system and an extension of the romanticized plantation life through a culture of song and narrative. The Ku Klux Klan worshipped on Sunday, populated local government offices on week day and made celebrated statements of hate through burning crosses, mass rallies and lynching as needed. Overt patterns of hatred and control were very familiar and well understood to those who were mistreated.

As the economy shifted, so did the immigration pattern of the formerly enslaved.[25] They became a new source of labor for a new part of the country. However, the American fiction remained true for the new metropolis as well. Regrettably, those who maintained the fiction often came to believe it and internalized it themselves. They would protect it with flag, gun and narrative. If it meant gang terrorism, whether in the form of spitting, beating, lynching, bombing, cursing, or raping the innocent, all could be justified and explained. The fiction could be maintained, but always with a degree of deniability and with unrecognized internal damage. White supremacy shrouded practices of sexual abuse and exploitation that were not only permitted, but increased the wealth of the slave legacy. Sexual harassment, safeguarding school systems through segregation and exploding incarceration rates became new forms of control. It was acceptable if it prevented the shift away from a dichotomous society.

Chapter 5
White Supremacy:
Psychopathology of Racism

The extreme racist behavior demonstrated during slavery, post-Reconstruction and the civil rights era can easily be analyzed through a lens of psychopathology. It is not normal or healthy to assault, kill, mutilate, rape or lynch in a healthy, well-adjusted personality. Psychologist, Dr. Bobby Wright was among the first to describe such racist behavior in terms of clinical psychopathology and mental disorder in 1974. He described the psychopath as having an absence of ethical and moral development, inability to experience guilt, inability to accept blame and a lack of concern with right and wrong behavior. "The psychopath is an individual who is constantly in conflict with other persons or groups. He is unable to experience guilt, is completely selfish and callous, and has a total disregard for the rights of others."[1] Couple this with the racist, who is defined in terms of power as one who participates in the "oppression and exploitation of people because of their race."[2] The psychopathic racial personality is one who would have the enduring traits common to mental health disorder manifest in abusing and exploiting others because of race.

Psychopathology is not normal. Even when such behavior is prevalent, its frequency does not make it healthy or normal. However, when such behavior is regarded as unacceptable, it is more typically categorized as criminal behavior. While racist acts can certainly be criminal, there can also be a mental health dynamic for the racist personality.[3] Such unhealthy behavior can occur among individuals who are conflicted and incomplete in their identity development. Their emotional problems can range from mild to severe. These personalities often demonstrate the capacity to cover or cloak unacceptable behavior with a socially acceptable façade. Power, charm or the capacity to place the blame on others permits the damaged personality to operate without resistance. Just as the bully on the playground knows when to hide his behavior and when to blame others, the racist psychopath develops an elaborate system for discharging unacceptable aggressive and sexual impulses. Over time, social constructs are developed which originate in these dysfunctional dynamics.

Hitler's great power did not emerge from healthy personality,[4] but as his power accumulated, there were few who would confront him[5] with his insecurity and life effort to compensate for his perceived inadequacy. Likewise, in the antebellum era, plantation wives, overseers and the enslaved all recognized the personality weaknesses in both presidents and planters alike, who failed to make moral or emotionally healthy

66

decisions. Being the child or wife of a disturbed racial personality generated additional dynamics of family confusion and dysfunction. Denial came to operate with additional ferocity. Biracial children may be accepted today, but they were evidence of hypocrisy, exploitation, and abuse in the antebellum South. Children who played with their biological half siblings soon became conditioned to either hate sexual immorality or to learn benefits of socially permitted impulse gratification.

Hiding immoral behavior produced another set of dysfunctional patterns. Rapists rarely struggle with incorporating their abusive behavior in healthy family, but instead over-rely on denial and compensation for their emotional inadequacy. Think about it. The sex offenders you know do not typically discuss conquests with family, but instead rely on a persona of innocence, which is masked with charm and prevarication. It is harder for children who have suspicion and for wives who recognize perversion. They too, come to over rely on denial. Sometimes, they may be able to create healthy lifestyle upon adulthood, but often the conflict that was unresolved for parent remains unresolved for offspring. It may be evident in competitive efforts to compensate and distract from painful realities. Materialism may be a compelling displacement for family members of unhealthy racist personalities. Wealth combined with white privilege quiets aggrieved family members.

Another coping mechanism for addressing dysfunctional family is over-identification with the power of the racist perpetrator. The pride taken in parent or husband dominates family relationship and often becomes a substitute for love; it serves as another aspect of denial. Complicating this dynamic further is the additional abuse and control that is required to hide shame-based secrets. Abuse that was confined to "acceptable" victims spills over into disrespect and abuse of family. Pedophilia, domestic violence and materialism confuse family members, yet often go unchecked, especially when power operates to compensate and cover maltreatment.

The widespread abuses of slavery have not been addressed in the white supremacist nor has the impact on their families or society been widely considered. African Americans have been far more ready to reclaim health by exploring the impact of enslavement on family health and survival. However, controlling psychopathic racial emotional disorder embedded in white America today is often unrecognized, denied and hidden. It can be characterized by narcissism, aggression, rigidity, lack of intimacy and inner fear. The presence of family dysfunction and emotional dysfunction is rarely studied as it relates to dynamics of racism and white privilege. While it is easier to identify racial psychopathology in the overt exploitation evident in Klan behavior and in self-proclaimed white supremacy, even here, it is often assessed in retrospect. Even with the resurgence of

68

white supremacist rhetoric, alt right media and neo-Nazi ideology, uneasiness makes it difficult to address the phenomenon as psychopathology while it is taking place. The foundation of historic denial makes it more difficult to recognize when it is not as overt and when personalities are assumed to be well intentioned.

For example, it is fairly simple to review American history and identify the racism and white supremacy reflected in custom and legal sanction. Yet, it is still painful for white America to accept the reality of her violent and exploitive past. Racism is poison for white personality and white family life. Amazingly, the toxin remains unadulterated with the evil, immoral outcome transmitted across generations.

The dimensions of racialized behavior are not confined to the extreme forms of racial hatred evident in Klan or Nazi practice. Such extreme behavior is dangerous not merely because of isolated instances of killings, taunting or vigilantism. It is dangerous because it normalizes less extreme, but more widespread dimensions of white privilege. It permits the false assumption that extremism is the totality of what white supremacy looks like.

Klan behavior in itself has the recognized impact of terrorism. Its less analyzed impact lies in its unifying use of symbols and with it, distraction from the larger, more subtle presence of maltreatment, which becomes normalized and accepted. Extreme racism represents an orientation anchored in declarations of ethnic superiority, which have permeated American society with sensational language and also with disorienting confusion and deniability. Its potent impact is twofold. First, it masks hidden racialized behavior in society and institution, which goes unchecked. In addition, it provides an opportunity for symbols to mobilize fringe elements with immunity. As powerful as the dynamics of racism and white supremacy are in American life, it is seldom consistently challenged, because it is cloaked with believable claims that it does not exist. If there is no racial epithet, if the Confederate flag is lowered and if the accepted symbols of racism morph into new, coded symbols, the dynamics of racism can operate with little opposition. The *Cuffee* of the Dred Scott Supreme Court decision is not an effective insult for today. The *nigger* of today may not be a meaningful degradation a century from now, but the need for insulting expressions of inferiorization will remain as long as racism as a social and personality dynamic is unchecked.

Mastery of this symbolic representation of oppression shifts over time. It may be the Nazi swastika or the Confederate flag. During the civil rights struggle, it was often the American flag itself. The American flag of forty-eight stars and even our current flag were often used as a sign of a patriotism that was consistent with the violence and repression of earlier patriots, who condemned Africans and Native Americans. As inflammatory as that might sound to white America, who experienced the symbol of the American flag in terms of its idealized history, it often

70

operated with a double meaning.[6] The American flag and the Confederate flag were often twin symbols for those invested in the American fiction where Black lives mattered only when they were deprived of voice and power. (And if you were an African American driving through the South in the Superman years, recognizing symbols was important for survival.[7])

White supremacy is often challenged in the aftermath of traumatic crisis. Guilt can be motivational. For example, with the forgiveness extended from survivors and family of the nine slain in Charleston, South Carolina at historic Emanuel AME Church on June 17, 2015, there was attention to the Confederate flag that flew over South Carolina state grounds.[8] It came down the next month, in reaction to the white supremacist assassin who took pride in posing with the Confederate symbol. Although this may have been an important victory for recognizing an inflammatory racial symbol, it was not a complete rejection of white supremacy and it was not a rejection of racism. It was an isolated rejection of what one symbol of racism means to many who have been victims. There was no change in the power dynamic and no recognition of the extent of its insidious nature. Lowering the flag was far easier than facing the introspection of what white privilege means for personal moral brokenness and ingrained personal fears. Few in white America would declare that the Confederate flag is treasonous. Its cultural embrace brings comfort from a historic American fiction and from the continuity that this fiction provides today.

White America has not only had white privilege, but it has had the amazing privilege of a protected practice of racial abuse and misuse. Because it has been too painful to explore, even mention of such effort is most typically dismissed and met with retreat. *There is no black America; there is no white America. There is just America.*[9] Out of context, that misconception effectively promotes the American fiction and at the same time, negates the African American voice. Thus, the need to consider racism as psychopathology and white supremacy as destructive for white personality is neutralized, and the dynamics affecting white family life remain relatively unaddressed. White supremacy continues to be emotionally immobilizing and is compensated with group denial and economic viability. There have been many studies of injustice and many calls for reconciliation, but rarely has there been attention to either the impact of hate or its denial on white family mental health.

The Trump Metaphor

On May 3, 2016, Donald Trump became the presumptive nominee of the Republican Party for the President of the United States in the 2016 election. The billionaire was familiar to Americans for his decade long reality television show, *The Apprentice,* which also promoted the many properties and holdings

72

branded with his name. Trump was able to maintain national media attention throughout his early candidacy with sensational insults of Mexicans, Muslims, women, the disabled, journalists, the Pope, and of course, President Obama. His bombastic criticisms of the Obama presidency were offensive and degrading, which is not unusual in political campaigns. However, Trump went further in building a loyal constituency by communicating xenophobic, misogynistic, and racist hope. Violence was not shunned in his rhetoric or his rallies. He remained careful not to distance himself from white nationalist leaders such as David Duke, whose vitriol against Jews could be more widely expressed. Between Trump's effective coded language of racial hate, his readiness to prevaricate and deny, and his team who defended him declaring that he would become presidential at the appropriate time, not enough Americans were willing to identify racism as a core appeal.

Trump did not lead with coded language, but with bold effrontery and outrageous, unrelenting insults.[10] This excited and mobilized his base. His easy to understand immigration policy of deportation of undocumented immigrants, building a wall on the Mexican border and denying Muslim access to America, along with his economic promise of more jobs, galvanized support at scores of large rallies throughout his campaign. His avid supporters were attracted to his bravado and his escalating rhetoric. His rise in the polls was surprising to pundits, who recognized his limited understanding of policy and his shocking pattern of agitation and contradiction.

Trump was divisive. At one point, he was alleged to have more Klan support than Republican support.[11] His divisiveness was so penetrating that the entire Republican Party was initially at risk of imploding. While Trump brought new people into the Republican fold, his core support remained the less educated, older and initially, white male demographic. His branding of rivals through the primaries with demeaning names (low-energy Jeb Bush, lyin' Ted Cruz, little Marco Rubio) appealed to less analytical, reactive followers. At last they could fight back and some did. Incidents of physical aggression at rallies were captured on social media.[12]

Yet, the question was repeatedly posed: what was the attraction of Donald Trump? Demagoguery was not new. It would be too simplistic to define him wholly in terms of an Obama racial backlash. Even though Trump pushed himself into the political arena with the birther movement[13] in an effort to discredit the legitimacy of President Obama by questioning his American birth and arrogantly demanding his documentation, the question of racism and white supremacy never gained traction as a significant explanation for his appeal. Yet, for many African Americans who saw in the birther assertion, the historic white citizen with the self-appointed power to declare superior, controlling position, the parallels were compelling. Echoes of the Dred Scott decision

74

(1857): "the black man was never meant to be a citizen and thus, has no rights the white man is bound to honor,"[14] were easily recognized. The birther would arbitrarily demand subservience, papers of freedom and in this case proof of citizenship, scholarship and permission.

What is significant about the ascendancy of Donald Trump is not merely what he said or tweeted. What is significant is how his comments connected with the unbroken link with America's past. His campaign rhetoric echoed a continuity with the history of American prosperity, which was built on polarized oppression. The timing of his anger-filled message, tempered with deniability and charm, cannot be understood apart from the presidency of African American Barack Obama, who excelled in statesmanship, temperament and character.

The country's response to Obama and Trump reflects the impasse of American racism. White America complained of perceived lost ground because of Obama while at the same time their desperate attempts to maintain white privilege surfaced with a frenzy around the possibility of a return to white power.

Trump can be understood as a metaphor for the contemporary American fiction. The Trump metaphor represents the arrogance, aggression, fear, hate and reckless power of white supremacy, which has always worked towards preserving racial structural inequity.

And there is always the component of an economic impetus: greed.

The Spectrum of White Supremacy

President Obama's brilliant legacy serves as catalyst for those vested in white dominance. The goal has become to diminish Obama's influence, create revisionist analysis of his accomplishments and punish his constituency even at the expense of the national good. This pattern of retribution at all costs was evident in the Civil War and can be traced to policies of repression that operate today. The detriment to the nation now ranges from gun violence to heroin epidemics in suburban communities. Yet, even though the analysis of racism through the African American lens can be pivotal in determining how to neutralize white supremacy and its new resurgence, it is ignored, while new ethnic targets are identified.

White supremacists can be characterized with the racialized psychopathology of moral disregard for others and focal conflict with others. The effort to secure and sustain superiority through blaming and condemning others often relates to the fragility of their psyche. At the core of white supremacy is not the power or greed that motivates, but it is always fear. White supremacists have personal and collective fear. Their threat and intimidation of others is an effective cover for internalized fear and limitation. The glee with which Trump supporters celebrate their chance to recover from perceived wrongs is often related to

76

unrecognized pain over identity and life struggles. It is hard to be unemployed, invisible, powerless and white. Trump raises a false hope that some of his millions will trickle down to white Americans and their pride can be restored. They believe he is capable of creating jobs, so his racist positions can be overlooked. Obama, who actually addressed the problems white supremacists name, is indicative that the stated problem is not the actual problem.

If overt racial abuse and verbal insult are at one end of the white supremacist spectrum, then on the other end is passivity, confusion and failure to address wrongdoing and its impact. White Americans who have compartmentalized views of white supremacy are typically disconnected from the lived experience of African Americans. They need not be hate-filled to have an attenuated form of white supremacy. They merely need to embrace enough denial that prevents them from seeing oppression and from hearing the voices of those who suffer. The great danger then becomes passive acceptance of a very widespread and deadly orientation.

Many Americans denounce the hate rhetoric of Trump and support the lowering of the Confederate flag. However, fewer are willing to address the underlying dynamic that operates personally and institutionally. *Trump was successful in tapping the anger of white Americans. Where does this anger interface with African American presence?*

When we return to the pattern of shooting unarmed African American men, it becomes impossible to integrate the dynamic of racism where there has been no readiness to consider its historic and contemporary role of community containment. Law enforcement operates very differently across communities. While affluent America is served and protected by police, the marginalized are automatically assumed to be criminal and at fault. The impasse in police/community relations remains frustrating with convoluted progress. Yet, the African American voice is never sought for meaningful solution. At best, high visibility collaborations, commissions and conferences followed by modification of practice occur so there is modification of behavioral acting out. Body cameras to decrease incidents of precipitous violence, anti-bias training to de-escalate conflict, and hiring more African American officers to decrease racial disparity are all efforts to change police culture. This is certainly important and it does make a difference.

However, the core of racial subordination and the systemic fueling of Black bodies for a prison economy must be more directly addressed. The institutionalized problem reflected in non-interrupted arrest rates of non-white men is rarely stressed and almost never addressed at the institutional level. Instead, there is the on-going effort to identify the problem at the isolated, individual level. This means that stereotype interfaces with isolated incident in a way that creates diversion from systemic process. There may be vindication

78

through the courts, civil settlement or modification of policy for isolated incidents of police shootings, but the institutional structure which promotes community occupation and epidemic incarceration rates remains untouched. Likewise, the attitudes which perpetuate institutional racial practices are permitted with no meaningful collective resistance.

Chapter 6
Persistence of the American Fiction

What will it take to face the American fiction of today? With such a harsh divide in the country, there appears to be little readiness to consider the solutions that can come from the African American community. The shift in the power dynamic has brought a return to controlling rigidity, which is hostile to the values of non-white communities. However, there now exists a critical number of Americans who are mobilized by the inclusion of the previously silenced African American voice. This new voice forcefully presents a painful reality to America: Black lives matter. The outcome of this work is as global today as it was during the Triangular Trade which generated profits from the enslaved. The Dred Scott Decision of 1857 now finds contemporary application to immigrants who have come to this country. The immigrant community of today is the new territory for containing, intimidating and controlling community.

The good news is that bridging the racial divide need not be as complicated as it may seem. The first step is to properly identify the problem. The corrective voice has always been present to do this and can be seen in cyclical peaks. From resistance to slave wealth to the freedom voices during the Civil War,

Reconstruction, Jim Crow, African American lynching and police killings, national attention has always been directed away from this message of truth and power. There has been a premature rush to healing with no fundamental changes at core. With a focus on superficial reconciliation, the emphasis has been on repressing or neutralizing conflict without attention to its institutional face. Thus, manifestation of the systemic problem reappears with a predictable effort to create a new version of the European fiction and to preserve the economic balance of power. Fear is fueled and manipulated to safeguard white power. However, the changing demographics of the nation (and now the world) make the corrective voice of the African American an important source for fuller understanding of racialized oppression and empowerment. This not only has implications for prevailing law enforcement and that place where community and law enforcement interface with unresolved killing of unarmed African American men and women. It also has implications for managing global racial and ethnic conflict. The American fiction persists and has become a microcosm of more global racialized oppression.

Today, there is overwhelming fear, confusion and disorientation where people of color meet the white citizen. The parallels are striking with a pervasive and reactive fear. *I am not a racist*. Yet, the fear of terrorism, unfamiliar culture and religion, and melanin (skin color) couple with fear of lost economic ground to create a familiar impasse. The white supremacist

82

appears with a neo-Nazi resurgence and also with normalized right-wing governance. While the politics in Europe and America cannot be reduced to a one dimensional consideration of the free movement of people, it would be a mistake to ignore the power dynamics related to people of color across the globe.

When there is successful definition of the problem and attention to institutional structure, tools for limiting racism and supremacist patterns can be more comprehensively addressed. Even if we fail to incorporate the African voice, it is not going away. On some level there already is a recognition of this African power base. It has contributed to a global counter-defiance, which re-energizes the alt right and presents white nationalists as victims—victims of liberal media, victims requiring safe spaces, victims of losing their entitled position. It is a futile position, but it represents a dangerous reality.

White supremacy does not work, but it can spread suddenly when conditions of fear are inflamed. Regrettably, it has re-surfaced as a global phenomenon[1] with reaction to changing immigration patterns, to terrorism and to expanding wealth gaps. But it does not work. Societal symptoms and underlying pathology must be recognized. In a day where bullying is denounced, the right to bear arms is sacrosanct, sexual abuse is epidemic and mental health is ostensibly pursued, there is conspicuous failure to evaluate the emotional damage secondary to hate and fear. Instead, it is covered with unconvincing declarations of innocence and with accumulating centers of power; and it is severely punished when the betrayal of the American fiction occurs. Politicians accused of racism may rant and curse in denouncing those accusations while the proof, which is evident in concrete behavior, documents convincingly. This defiant protest of the white nationalist can be traced back to the betrayal of the idealized American fiction which remains divorced from fact and reality. America is a rich nation, but the cost for white privilege in human capital has been extraordinary. Violence, apathy, greed and arrogance require a steady fuel of exploited bodies in the name of compromised ideals, be it *law and order* or *Make America Great Again.* Without the catalyst of racism, the bodies cannot be forthcoming. Yet, this process can only be time limited.

The corrective African American voice disrupts a patriotism that is not fully patriotic and a religiosity that does not honor God. It exposes immediate issues of state sanctioned violence against African American men (and women), as well as wider practices of injustice, which permeate community and nation. The bodies that have fueled the economy of white supremacy are now represented in voice to question and challenge illegal and abusive practices. Here there emerges a previously dismissed power, which has solution for the failed policies of division and hate. Even though there has been a vast power conglomerate which has evolved outside of government and has

84

benefited from policies of exploitation and abuse, there has also been a counterbalance concentrated in youth and new constituencies. Those maligned and *othered* function to assert power with the potential of offering new paradigms of solution.

As the world continues to change dramatically, millennials are less concerned with racial compartmentalization.[2] Social media introduces unprecedented opportunity to understand and eradicate injustice. While improved communication has often served to promote destructive practices, it also represents new perceptions of the lingering patterns of social disparity. White people are discovering that they are not necessarily white (according to available DNA testing). There is a new, more open recognition of racial reality. At the same time, while there remains competing frustration at a shifting world order which no longer preserves white privilege, there is counter messaging. The enduring American legacy of white supremacy as reflected in the African American narrative has powerful opportunity for more global application. Painfully, African Americans have not been the only marginalized group in the nation. However, the history of Africans in America, not only provides voice, but offers a profound perspective for more global solution.

Dismantling of this false value system of white superiority must be replaced with an energized, sometimes radicalized, insistence that a new narrative of fairness be operative. The white man, angry over

85

losing ground because of racial heritage, has been seen in this country before. Today we again have the opportunity to revisit, to analyze and to resolve. The conflict between white America and African American citizen offers renewed opportunity to secure authentic justice. It has important application for global resolutions and for understanding the racial and religious dynamics that appear across Europe and Asia. If we choose to bridge the racial divide in our nation, we can become that nation we say we are. This time the voices that ring out must also include leadership from the voices of freedom that are reclaimed from their narrative of oppression. The world needs this power and it can only be recovered from the authority of those who have been marginalized and ignored.

Emmitt Till's death was pivotal for the nation's civil rights transformation, but freedoms that were begun in this country were echoed in colonial resistance and liberation throughout Africa. Other marginalized groups have also benefited from the African American fight for justice. Likewise, we must insist that the innocent African American lives slain across the country in incidents of police violence have not lost their lives in vain.

Just as Emmitt Till's death transformed the politics of liberation, consider Alton Sterling, Philando Castile, Michael Brown, Eric Garner, Freddie Gray, Walter Scott, Tamir Rice, and Oscar Grant. Consider also Trayvon Martin, Jordan Davis and Clinton Allen along with the women slain at the hands of police: Rekia

Boyd, Miriam Carey, Tanisha Anderson, Yvette Smith, Eula Love and also Etta Collins, Renisha McBride and Sandra Bland. Approximately twenty percent of unarmed African Americans killed by police are women. These scores of deaths are a precious catalyst for the transformation that the world needs today. With the global resurgence of fear, terrorism and immigration patterns, the African American voice is a powerful voice that must help redeem the world from its politics of fear and hate.

"You know, and I know, that the country is celebrating one hundred years of freedom one hundred years too soon. We cannot be free until they are free."

James Baldwin on the One Hundredth Anniversary of the Emancipation

Acknowledgements

This succinct volume was made possible by the encouragement and support of many. It is my great joy to thank Dr. David Wall Rice, who always inspires and his wonderful wife, Mikki Harris, who is always available with photographic support and love. My earliest encouragement came from Cassie Harris, who shared articles, when all of us were so overwhelmed by grief and repeated tragedy. I must thank Dr. Jean Robinson Casey and her dear husband, Rev. Clyde Casey for their prayers and love. The surprising joy was my reconnection with Emily M. Newsome. She is the poet who edited, researched, re-edited and prayed.

Thank you all.

Notes

1   Reynolds, Lavish. "Transcript of Video in Philando Castile Shooting." Minnesota.cbslocal.com. http://minnesota.cbslocal.com/2016/07/07/transcript-of-facebook-video-in-philando-castile-shooting/

Heartbreak

1   Richmond, Kait. "Philando Castile's mother: "He was black in the wrong place." CNN. http://www.cnn.com/2016/07/07/us/philando-castile-family-new-day/

2   Irvine, Chris and Graham, Regina F. "'Would this have happened if the passenger were white,': Minnesota governor decries police racism after cop shoots dead black man in his car." Daily Mail. http://www.dailymail.co.uk/news/article-3679761/Would-happened-passengers-white-don-t-think-Minnesota-governor-decries-police-racism-cop-shoots-dead-black-man-car.html

3   Reynolds, Lavish. "Transcript of Video in Philando Castile Shooting."Minnesota.cbslocal.com. http://minnesota.cbslocal.com/2016/07/07/transcript-of-facebook-video-in-philando-castile-shooting/

4   Irvine, Chris and Graham, Regina F. "'Would this have happened if the passenger were white,': Minnesota governor decries police

racism after cop shoots dead black man in his car." Daily Mail. http://www.dailymail.co.uk/news/article-3679761/Would-happened-passengers-white-don-t-think-Minnesota-governor-decries-police-racism-cop-shoots-dead-black-man-car.html

5   *Ibid.*

6   Garunay, Melanie. "President Obama on the Fatal Shooting of Alton Sterling and Philando Castile." Obama White House Archives. https://obamawhitehouse.archives.gov/blog/2016/07/07/president-obama-fatal-shootings-alton-sterling-and-philando-castile

7   Fernandez, Manny; Perez-Pena, Richard and Bromwich, Jonah Engel. "Five Dallas Officers Were Killed as Payback, Police Chief Says." The New York Times. https://www.nytimes.com/2016/07/09/us/dallas-police-shooting.html?_r=0

8   Newton-Small, Jay. "Falsely Accused, Dallas 'Suspect' Now Fears for His Life." Time.com. http://time.com/4399697/dallas-shooting-mark-hughes-false-suspect/

9   Liptak, Kevin. "Obama on Dallas: 'Vicious, calculated, despicable attack on law enforcement.'" CNN.com. http://www.cnn.com/2016/07/08/politics/obama-dallas-police-shootings/

10   Fernandez, Manny; Perez-Pena, Richard and Bromwich, Jonah Engel. "Five Dallas Officers Were Killed as Payback, Police Chief Says." NYTimes.com.

https://www.nytimes.com/2016/07/09/us/dallas-police-shooting.html?_r=0

11 Maclauchlan, Shawn. "WATCH LIVE: Prayer vigil for Dallas Police at Thanksgiving Square." NBC12.com. http://www.nbc12.com/story/32401365/watch-live-prayer-vigil-for-dallas-police-at-thanksgiving-square

12 Silverstein, Jason. "Former Illinois Rep. Joe Walsh threatens 'war' on Obama and Black Lives Matter protesters, blames them for deaths after Dallas attack." NYDailyNews.com. http://www.nydailynews.com/news/national/joe-walsh-war-obama-black-lives-matter-dallas-article-1.2703883

13 "U.S. Capitol, Visitor Center Briefly Placed on Lockdown as Police Investigated 'Person of Interest.'" KTLA.com. http://ktla.com/2016/07/08/u-s-capitol-visitor-center-on-lockdown-as-police-investigate-person-of-interest/

14 "Army reservist who killed 5 Dallas officers showed symptoms of PTSD." CBSNews.com. http://www.cbsnews.com/news/army-reservist-who-killed-5-dallas-officers-showed-symptoms-of-ptsd/

15 "Black Lives Matter condemns Dallas, pushes forward with protests." CBSNews.com. http://www.cbsnews.com/news/dallas-shooting-black-lives-matter-leaders-respond/

16 Gottfried, Mara, Verges, Josh, Melo, Frederick, Vezner, Tad and Rathbun, Andy. "After weekend violence, Philando Castile's family calls for calm." www.twincities.com.

http://www.twincities.com/2016/07/09/amid-racial-strife-hundreds-seek-answers-in-protests-church-service/

17 "100+ arrested in weekend Baton Rouge protests." q13fox.com. http://q13fox.com/2016/07/10/100-arrested-in-weekend-baton-rouge-protests/

18 O'Sullivan, Mike. "Obama: 'I Firmly Believe America is Not as Divided as Some Have Suggested.'" www.voanews.com. http://www.voanews.com/a/shooting-in-dallas/3408984.html

19 Sanburn, Josh. "Philando Castile Shooting Had 'Nothing to Do With Race,' Officer's Attorney Says."

Chapter 1 – Establishing Context

1 "Shooting of Michael Brown." en.wikipedia.org. https://en.wikipedia.org/wiki/Shooting_of_Michael_Brown

2 *Ibid.*

3 *Ibid.*

4 Gruttadaro, Andrew. "Ferguson Police Trampled a Michael Brown Memorial After Letting Their Dogs Pee on It." www.complex.com. http://www.complex.com/pop-culture/2014/08/ferguson-police-desecrate-michael-brown-memorial

5 Reilly, Ryan J. "'Provocative' Police Tactics Inflamed Ferguson Protests, Experts Find."

www.huffingtonpost.com.
http://www.huffingtonpost.com/entry/ferguson-protests-police-tactics-report_us_55e622a3e4b0aec9f35506ad

6 Bouie, Jamelle. "The Militarization of the Police." www.slate.com.
http://www.slate.com/articles/news_and_politic s/politics/2014/08/police_in_ferguson_military_weapons_threaten_protesters.html

7 Malek, Alia and Dizard Wilson. "DOJ says Ferguson police violated African-Americans' free speech rights." America.aljazeera.com.
http://america.aljazeera.com/articles/2015/3/4/J ustice-says-Ferguson-police-violated-1st-amendment-rights.html

8 Verton, Dan. "DHS grant programs come under scrutiny in aftermath of Ferguson riots." www.fedscoop.com.
https://www.fedscoop.com/police-militarization-has-roots-in-dhs-grant-programs-not-pentagon/

9 Alcindor, Yamiche. Police defend tactics during Michael Brown unrest." www.usatoday.com.
http://www.usatoday.com/story/news/nation/20 14/08/27/ferguson-police-missouri-michael-brown/14710497/

10 Bruce, Betsey, Smith, Chris and KTVIDScruggs. "State of Emergency: Nixon imposes curfew in Ferguson." Fox2news.com.
http://fox2now.com/2014/08/16/governor-nixon-imposes-curfew-in-the-city-of-ferguson-midnight-5am/

11 "Amnesty International Releases New

Ferguson Report Documenting Human Rights Abuses." www.amnestyusa.org.
http://www.amnestyusa.org/news/press-releases/amnesty-international-releases-new-ferguson-report-documenting-human-rights-abuses

12 "Michael Brown Funeral Filled With Calls to Action for Justice." www.bet.com.
http://www.bet.com/news/national/2014/08/25/watch-the-live-stream-of-michael-brown-s-memorial-service.html

13 Kohler, Jeremy. "Statement of St. Louis Prosecuting Attorney Robert P. McCulloch." www.stltoday.com.
http://www.stltoday.com/news/local/crime-and-courts/statement-of-st-louis-prosecuting-attorney-robert-p-mcculloch/article_2becfef3-9b4b-5e1e-9043-f586f389ef91.html

14 Crouch, Elisa. "Michael Brown remembered as a 'gentle giant.'" www.stltoday.com.
http://www.stltoday.com/news/local/crime-and-courts/michael-brown-remembered-as-a-gentle-giant/article_cbafa12e-7305-5fd7-8e0e-3139f472d130.html

15 "United States' Compliance with the Convention Against Torture and Other Cruel, Inhuman or Degrading Treatment or Punishment: Written Statement on the Police Shooting of Michael Brown and Ensuing Police Violence Again Protestors in Ferguson, Missouri. 53rd Session of the United Nations Committee Against Torture. November 3-28, 2014."
http://i2.cdn.turner.com/cnn/2014/images/11/11

/fergusonreport.pdf

16 "NYPD chokehold death of Eric Garner was homicide: medical examiner." Nydailynews.com. http://video.nydailynews.com/NYPD-chokehold-death-of-Eric-Garner-was-homicide-medical-examiner-26476239

17 Fisher, Ian. "Kelly Bans Choke Holds By Officers." www.nytimes.com. http://www.nytimes.com/1993/11/24/nyregion/kelly-bans-choke-holds-by-officers.html

18 Tetteh, Michaelene. "Part 2 Video UNCUT Eric Garner THE AFTERMATH. NYPD Puts Asthmatic Man in a Chokehold." www.youtube.com. https://www.youtube.com/watch?v=5z3sHLHuAQM

19 Siff, Andrew, Dienst, Jonathan and Millman, Jennifer. "Grand Jury Declines to Indict NYPD Officer in Eric Garner Chokehold Death." www.nbcnewyork.com. http://www.nbcnewyork.com/news/local/Grand-Jury-Decision-Eric-Garner-Staten-Island-Chokehold-Death-NYPD-284595921.html

20 Goodman, J. David and Baker, Al. "Wave of Protests After Grand Jury Doesn't Indict Officer in Eric Garner Chokehold Case." www.nytimes.com. https://www.nytimes.com/2014/12/04/nyregion/grand-jury-said-to-bring-no-charges-in-staten-island-chokehold-death-of-eric-garner.html?_r=0

21 "Tamir Rice: police release video of 12-year-old's fatal shooting – video." The Guardian.

https://www.theguardian.com/us-
news/video/2014/nov/26/cleveland-video-
tamir-rice-shooting-police

22 "Cleveland police handcuff Tamir Rice's sister
after shooting 12-year-old video."
www.theguardian.com.
https://www.theguardian.com/us-
news/video/2015/jan/08/new-video-tamir-rice-
shooting-sister-video

23 "Tamir Rice's mother: son shot before he could
comply with police orders."
www.theguardian.com.
https://www.theguardian.com/us-
news/2014/dec/15/tamir-rice-mother-shot-
police-orders

24 Schultz, Connie. "A City of Two Tales."
www.politico.com.
http://www.politico.com/magazine/story/2015/
02/tamir-rice-cleveland-police-
115401_Page3.html#.WNFlRlXyuUk

25 Shaffer, Cory. "Tamir Rice decision: No
indictments of Cleveland police officers."
www.cleveland.com.
http://www.cleveland.com/metro/index.ssf/201
5/12/tamir_rice_decision_no_indictm.html

26 Ford, Matt. "Shot and Killed While Running
Away."
https://www.theatlantic.com/politics/archive/20
15/04/shot-and-killed-while-running-
away/389976/

27 United States Supreme Court. "Graham vs.
Connor, (1989), No. 87-6571 Argued: February
21, 1989 Decided: May 15, 1989."
Caselaw.findlaw.com.

http://caselaw.findlaw.com/us-supreme-court/490/386.html

28 Knapp, Andrew. "Scott family: Charge a 'turning point.'" www.postandcourier.com. http://www.postandcourier.com/archives/scott-family-charge-a-turning-point/article_81be2c8d-8271-5310-a652-7cb4bb6a2e08.html

29 Jackson, Jerry. Baltimore Sun. www.dailymail.com. "Disturbing video shows BPD drag Freddie Gray during arrest." http://www.dailymail.co.uk/video/news/video-1176745/Baltimore-Police-drag-Freddie-Gray-van-arrest.html

30 "Freddie Gray's death in police custody – what we know." www.bbc.com. http://www.bbc.com/news/world-us-canada-32400497

31 Stolberg, Sheryl Gay. "Police Officers Charged in Freddie Gray's Death to be Tried in Baltimore." www. Nytimes.com. https://www.nytimes.com/2015/09/11/us/freddie-gray-trial-baltimore.html?_r=0

32 "Freddie Gray autopsy: excerpt from the report." www.baltimoresun.com. http://www.baltimoresun.com/news/maryland/freddie-gray/bal-read-the-freddie-gray-autopsy-report-text-story.html

33 Collman, Ashley. "Freddie Gray was 'intentionally trying to injure himself in van', claims leaked police report that quotes anonymous prisoner." www.dailymail.co.uk. http://www.dailymail.co.uk/news/article-3061882/Freddie-Gray-intentionally-trying-

injure-prisoner-rode-van-claims-leaked-police-report.html

34 Friedersdorf, Conor. "The Brutality of Police Culture in Baltimore." www.theatlantic.com. https://www.theatlantic.com/politics/archive/2015/04/the-brutality-of-police-culture-in-baltimore/391158/

35 Yan, Holly and Ford, Dana. "Baltimore riots: Looting, fires engulf city after Freddie Gray's funeral." www.cnn.com. http://www.cnn.com/2015/04/27/us/baltimore-unrest/

36 Fenton, Justin and Green, Erica L. "Baltimore rioting kicked off with rumors of 'purge'." www.baltimoresun.com. http://www.baltimoresun.com/news/maryland/freddie-gray/bs-md-ci-freddie-gray-violence-chronology-20150427-story.html

37 WMAR Staff. "Mayor Stephanie Rawlings-Blake: Wants all officers charged in Gray case suspended." www.abc2news.com. http://www.abc2news.com/news/region/baltimore-city/live-1-mayor-stephanie-rawlings-blake-to-react-to-officer-indictments-in-freddie-gray-case

38 Capehart, Jonathan. "Marilyn Mosby's amazing press conference." www.washingtonpost.com. https://www.washingtonpost.com/blogs/post-partisan/wp/2015/05/01/marilyn-mosbys-amazing-press-conference/?utm_term=.1850997800c7

39 Wenger, Yvonne and Puente, Mark. "Baltimore to pay Freddie Gray's family $6.4 million to

settle civil claims." www.baltimoresun.com.
http://www.baltimoresun.com/news/maryland/f
reddie-gray/bs-md-ci-boe-20150908-story.html
40 Rector, Kevin. "Charges dropped, Freddie Gray
case concludes with zero convictions against
officers." www.baltimoresun.com.
http://www.baltimoresun.com/news/maryland/f
reddie-gray/bs-md-ci-miller-pretrial-motions-
20160727-story.html

Chapter 2 – Post Racial Society Becomes Racial

1 Cho, Sumi. "Post-racialism." Iowa Law
Review. 94.5. July 2009. P1589.
http://go.galegroup.com.proxy.libraries.smu.ed
u/ps/i.do?p=AONE&u=txshracd2548&id=GAL
E|A208129843&v=2.1&it=r&sid=summon&au
thCount=1
2 Cogburn, Derrick L. and Espinoza-Vasquez,
Fatima K. "From Networked Nominee to
Networked Nation: Examining the Impact of
Web 2.0 and Social Media on Political
Participation and Civic Engagement in the
2008 Obama Campaign." Taylor & Francis
Online. www.tandfonline.com.
http://www.tandfonline.com/doi/abs/10.1080/1
5377857.2011.540224
3 *Ibid.*
4 Wallace, Gregory. "Inauguration brings
different kind of gridlock to D.C."
www.cnn.com.
http://www.cnn.com/2013/01/16/politics/inaug
uration-security/index.html

5   Capehart, Jonathan. "Republicans had it in for
     Obama before Day 1."
     www.washingtonpost.com.
     https://www.washingtonpost.com/blogs/post-
     partisan/post/republicans-had-it-in-for-obama-
     before-day-1/2012/08/10/0c96c7c8-e31f-11e1-
     ae7f-
     d2a13e249eb2_blog.html?utm_term=.d2038b3
     1f76e
6   Beasley, J. Thomas. "Obama's Legacy: Most
     Disrespected President Ever."
     www.yourlawscholar.com.
     http://www.yourlawscholar.com/obamas-
     legacy-most-disrespected-president-ever/
7   U.S. Bureau of Labor Statistics.
     https://data.bls.gov/pdq/SurveyOutputServlet
8   "Congress' Job Approval 19% at Start of New
     Session." www.gallup.com.
     http://www.gallup.com/poll/201974/congress-
     job-approval-start-new-session.aspx
9   Pitney, Nico. "This Is What Actual Voter
     Suppression Looks Like And It's Appalling."
     www.huffingtonpost.com.
     http://www.huffingtonpost.com/entry/voter-
     suppression-
     2016_us_581028c2e4b02b1d9e63bcd2
10   Badger, Emily. "12 Very Real Voter-
     Suppression Tactics Experts Now Worry Will
     Come Back." www.citylab.com.
     http://www.citylab.com/politics/2013/06/12-
     very-real-voter-suppression-tactics-experts-
     now-worry-will-come-back/6057/
11   Liptak, Adam. "Supreme Court Upholds Health
     Care Law, 5-4, in Victory for Obama.

www.nytimes.com.
http://www.nytimes.com/2012/06/29/us/suprem
e-court-lets-health-law-largely-stand.html

12 "Congress' Job Approval 19% at Start of New
Session." www.gallup.com.
http://www.gallup.com/poll/201974/congress-
job-approval-start-new-session.aspx

13 Amadeo, Kimberly. "What Was Obama's
Stimulus Package?" www.thebalance.com.
https://www.thebalance.com/what-was-obama-
s-stimulus-package-3305625

14 Ahamed, Liaquat. "Obama's Wall Street Bank
Rescue Stabilized Economy at a Political
Cost." www.bloomberg.com.
https://www.bloomberg.com/news/articles/201
3-09-12/obamas-wall-street-bank-rescue-
stabilized-economy-at-a-political-cost

15 Greenberg, Jon. "Did President Obama save the
auto industry?" www.politifact.com.
http://www.politifact.com/truth-o-
meter/article/2012/sep/06/did-obama-save-us-
automobile-industry/

16 Phillips, Macon. "Osama Bin Laden Dead."
Obamawhitehouse.archives.gov.
https://obamawhitehouse.archives.gov/blog/201
1/05/02/osama-bin-laden-dead

17 "Remarks by the President on Ending the War
in Iraq." Obamawhitehouse,archives,gov.
https://obamawhitehouse.archives.gov/the-
press-office/2011/10/21/remarks-president-
ending-war-iraq

18 Debusmann, Bernd. "After Two Terms of
Obama, a Post-Racial America is Still Elusive."
www.newsweek.com.

http://www.newsweek.com/after-two-terms-obama-post-racial-america-still-elusive-506916

19 Higgins, Eoin. "The White Backlash to the Civil Rights Movement." Eoinhiggins.com. https://eoinhiggins.com/the-white-backlash-to-the-civil-rights-movement-1817ff0a9fc

20 Blake, John. "Who will you blame once Obama's gone?" www.cnn.com. http://www.cnn.com/2015/11/27/us/obama-race-cnn-kff-poll/

21 Lundegaard, Erik. "Truth, Justice and (Fill in the Blank)." www.nytimes.com. http://www.nytimes.com/2006/06/30/opinion/30lundegaard.html

22 Shapiro, Emily. "Superheroes Are 'Like Cops,' Dallas Police Chief Says in Powerful Speech." www.abcnews.com. http://abcnews.go.com/US/superheroes-cops-dallas-police-chief-powerful-speech/story?id=40511457

23 Washburn, Wilcomb E., "Indians and the American Revolution." www.Americanrevoultion.org. http://www.americanrevolution.org/ind1.php

24 "Greenville Slogan on Card Intrigued Wilson." The USGenWeb Project. http://www.rootsweb.ancestry.com/~txhunt/GreenvilleSign.html

25 Jensen, Erik M. "Three-fifths Clause." The Heritage Guide to the Constitution. http://www.heritage.org/constitution#!/articles/1/essays/6/three-fifths-clause

26 "Christianity as a Justification for Slavery." The History Engine.

http://historyengine.richmond.edu/episodes/view/3535

27 "Economy in the American Revolution."
Shmoop.com.
http://www.shmoop.com/american-revolution/economy.html

28 "Christianity as a Justification for Slavery."
The History Engine.
http://historyengine.richmond.edu/episodes/view/3535

29 Stadler, Jan. "The Founding Fathers Revisited,
Part 2: The Creation of the United States and
the Establishment of White Supremacy."
Faithandheritage.com.
http://faithandheritage.com/2014/03/the-founding-fathers-revisited-part-2-the-creation-of-the-united-states-and-the-establishment-of-white-supremacy/

30 Drake, Bruce. "Incarceration gap widens
between whites and blacks." Pew Research
Center. http://www.pewresearch.org/fact-tank/2013/09/06/incarceration-gap-between-whites-and-blacks-widens/

31 "'Huckleberry Finn' and the N-Word Debate."
60 Minutes.
http://www.cbsnews.com/news/huckleberry-finn-and-the-n-word-debate/

32 "Statistics About Sexual Violence." National
Sexual Violence Resource Center-Info & Stats
for Journalists.
http://www.nsvrc.org/sites/default/files/publications_nsvrc_factsheet_media-packet_statistics-about-sexual-violence_0.pdf

33 Humphrey, Bill. "The U.S. Torture Report and

White Supremacy." The Globalist.
https://www.theglobalist.com/the-u-s-torture-report-and-white-supremacy/

34 Victor, Daniel. "Why 'All Lives Matter' Is Such a Perilous Phrase." New York Times. https://www.nytimes.com/2016/07/16/us/all-lives-matter-black-lives-matter.html?_r=0

Chapter 3 – American Racism and White Supremacy

1 Thompson, Tracy. "The South still lies about the Civil War." Salon. http://www.salon.com/2013/03/16/the_south_still_lies_about_the_civil_war/

2 Jefferson, Thomas. Shuffelton, Frank editor. Notes on the State of Virginia. (First published in France 1785.) Penguin Books. 1999.

3 "Jefferson's Ancestry." Thomas Jefferson Foundation. https://www.monticello.org/site/research-and-collections/jeffersons-ancestry

4 "Sally Hemings." Thomas Jefferson Foundation, Inc. https://www.monticello.org/site/plantation-and-slavery/sally-hemings

5 Pompeian, Ed. "George Washington's Slave Child?" Columbia College of Arts & Sciences History News Network. http://historynewsnetwork.org/article/10827

6 Curtis, Mary C. "Strom Thurmond's black daughter: a symbol of America's complicated racial history." The Washington Post.

https://www.washingtonpost.com/blogs/she-the-people/wp/2013/02/05/strom-thurmonds-black-daughter-a-flesh-and-blood-symbol-of-americas-complicated-racial-history/?utm_term=.63e1e97ab7d8

7   Sambol-Tosco, Kimberly. "The Slave Experience: Legal Rights and Government." PBS: Slavery and the Making of America. http://www.pbs.org/wnet/slavery/experience/legal/history.html

8   "Fugitive Slave Acts: United States [1793, 1850]" Encyclopedia Britannica. https://www.britannica.com/event/Fugitive-Slave-Acts

9   "The case of Dred Scott in the United States Supreme Court. The full opinions of Chief Justice Taney and Justice Curtis, and abstracts of the opinions of the other judges; with an analysis of the points rule, and some concluding observations." Library of Congress. https://www.loc.gov/resource/llst.020/?st=gallery

10 *Ibid.*

11 Plessy v. Ferguson 163 U.S. 537 (1896). Justia US Supreme Court. https://supreme.justia.com/cases/federal/us/163/537/case.html.

12 Pilgrim, David. "What was Jim Crow." Ferris State University Jim Crow Museum of Racist Memorabilia. http://www.ferris.edu/jimcrow/what.htm/

13 Brown v. Board of Education of Topeka 347 U.S. 483 (1954). Justia US Supreme Court.

https://supreme.justia.com/cases/federal/us/347/483/case.html.

14 Frederickson, Kari. "Dixiecrats." Encyclopedia of Alabama. http://www.encyclopediaofalabama.org/article/h-1477

15 "Battle Flags of the Army of Northern Virginia." War Flags Showcase Confederate States of America. http://tmg110.tripod.com/usarmyh9.htm

16 "The Ku Klux Klan." Digital History ID 3386. http://www.digitalhistory.uh.edu/disp_textbook.cfm?smtid=2&psid=3386

17 "Compromise of 1877." History.com. http://www.history.com/topics/us-presidents/compromise-of-1877

18 Pilgrim, David. "Jim Crow Museum of Racist Memorabilia." Ferris State University. http://www.ferris.edu/jimcrow/what.htm/

19 Greene, Jamal and McAward, Jennifer Mason. "The Thirteenth Amendment." Common Interpretation – Constitution Center. https://constitutioncenter.org/interactive-constitution/amendments/amendment-xiii

20 Pilgrim, David. "Jim Crow Museum of Racist Memorabilia." Ferris State University. http://www.ferris.edu/jimcrow/what.htm/

21 Frederickson, Kari. "Dixiecrats." Encyclopedia of Alabama. http://www.encyclopediaofalabama.org/article/h-1477

22 Sterling, Joe. "White nationalism, a term once on the fringes, now front and center." CNN.com.

http://www.cnn.com/2016/11/16/politics/what-is-white-nationalism-trnd/index.html

23 Mimh, Stephen. "Where slavery thrived, inequality rules today." Boston Globe. https://www.bostonglobe.com/ideas/2014/08/23/where-slavery-thrived-inequality-rules-today/iF5zgFsXncPoYmYCMMs67J/story.html

24 Horton, James. "Q: How did slavery affect free black people and white people?" Judgment Day-Part4: 1831-1865. Africans in America. Resource Bank. http://www.pbs.org/wgbh/aia/part4/4i3104.html

25 Applebaum, Barbara. "Critical Whiteness Studies." Education Oxford Research Encyclopedias. http://education.oxfordre.com/view/10.1093/acrefore/9780190264093.001.0001/acrefore-9780190264093-e-5

26 McIntosh, Peggy. "White Privilege: Unpacking The Invisible Knapsack." From Multiculturalism. Complied by Filor, Anna May. New York Stat Council on Educational Associations. 1992. pp 30-36. ERIC. http://files.eric.ed.gov/fulltext/ED355141.pdf#page=43

27 Applebaum, Barbara. "Critical Whiteness Studies." Education Oxford Research Encyclopedias. http://education.oxfordre.com/view/10.1093/acrefore/9780190264093.001.0001/acrefore-9780190264093-e-5

28 Chediac, Joyce. "Punishment for profit: The economics of mass incarceration." Workers

World.
http://www.workers.org/2015/05/04/punishmen
t-for-profit-the-economics-of-mass-
incarceration/#.WQlICNLys_M
29 Dayden, David. "African-Americans Are Still
Being Victimized by the Mortgage Market."
New Republic.
https://newrepublic.com/article/117912/reparati
ons-how-mortgage-market-hurts-african-
americans
30 Sledge, Matt. "The Drug War And Mass
Incarceration By The Numbers." The
Huffington Post.
http://www.huffingtonpost.com/2013/04/08/dru
g-war-mass-incarceration_n_3034310.html
31 McIntosh, Peggy. "White Privilege: Unpacking
The Invisible Knapsack." From
Multiculturalism. Complied by Filor, Anna
May. New York Stat Council on Educational
Associations. 1992. pp 30-36. ERIC.
http://files.eric.ed.gov/fulltext/ED355141.pdf#p
age=43
32 Zangrando, Robert L. "About Lynching."
Modern American Poetry.
http://www.english.illinois.edu/maps/poets/g_l/
lynching/lynching.htm
33 Callahan, John F. "About Lynching." Modern
American Poetry.
http://www.english.illinois.edu/maps/poets/g_l/
lynching/lynching.htm
34 "Emmett Till murderers make magazine
confession." This Day in History: Jan 24, 1956.
History. http://www.history.com/this-day-in-
history/emmett-till-murderers-make-magazine-

confession

Chapter 4 – Black Lives Matter

1 "Race and the Drug War." Drug Policy Alliance. http://www.drugpolicy.org/race-and-drug-war

2 Lo Bianco, Tom. "Report: Aide says Nixon's war on drugs targeted blacks, hippies." CNN. http://www.cnn.com/2016/03/23/politics/john-ehrlichman-richard-nixon-drug-war-blacks-hippie/

3 Metta, John. "Why I Don't Talk About Race With White People." Alternet. http://www.alternet.org/civil-liberties/why-i-dont-talk-about-race-white-people

4 Blake, John. "The new threat: 'Racism without racists.'" CNN. http://www.cnn.com/2014/11/26/us/ferguson-racism-or-racial-bias/

5 Wing, Nick. "When The Media Treats White Suspects and Killers Better Than Black Victims." Huffington Post. http://www.huffingtonpost.com/2014/08/14/media-black-victims_n_5673291.html

6 Bevens, Donna K. "What is Internalized Racism?" Chapter 5 of Flipping the Script: White Privilege and Community Building, pp. 43-51. http://www.racialequitytools.org/resourcefiles/What_is_Internalized_Racism.pdf

7 Zeilinger, Julie. "This New Study Explains Why White People Deny Their Privilege." Mic

Network Inc.
https://mic.com/articles/122149/new-study-explains-the-denial-of-white-privilege#.pwQxMdsjm

8   "Resolution on Racial Reconciliation On The 150th Anniversary Of the Southern Baptist Convention." Southern Baptist Convention. http://www.sbc.net/resolutions/899/resolution-on-racial-reconciliation-on-the-150th-anniversary-of-the-southern-baptist-convention

9   "H.Res. 194 (110th): Apologizing for the enslavement and racial segregation of African-Americans." GovTrack. https://www.govtrack.us/congress/bills/110/hres194/text

10 Douglas, William. "Congress' apology for slavery just proves it's hard to say sorry." McClatchy DC Bureau. http://www.mcclatchydc.com/news/politics-government/article24544429.html

11 "Black code." Encyclopedia Britannica. https://www.britannica.com/topic/black-code

12 Pettit, Becky. "Mass imprisonment and the life course: Race and class inequality in U.S. incarceration." American sociological review, Vol. 69. ISSN: 0003-1224. 2004. pp 151-169. http://sc2xx8ju8d.search.serialssolutions.com.proxy.libraries.smu.edu/?sid=sage&iuid=305219&aulast=Pettit%2C+Becky&aulast=Bruce+Western.&date=2004&atitle=Mass+imprisonment+and+the+life+course%3A+Race+and+class+inequality+in+U.S.+incarceration&title=American+Sociological+Review&volu

13 Mitrani, Sam. "The Police Were Created to

Control Working Class and Poor People, Not 'Serve and Protect.'" In These Times. http://inthesetimes.com/working/entry/17505/police_and_poor_people

14 "Police Presence in Schools." American Civil Liberties Union. https://www.aclu.org/issues/juvenile-justice/school-prison-pipeline/police-presence-schools

15 Capehart, Jonathan. "Republicans had it in for Obama before Day 1." The Washington Post. https://www.washingtonpost.com/blogs/post-partisan/post/republicans-had-it-in-for-obama-before-day-1/2012/08/10/0c96c7c8-e31f-11e1-ae7f-d2a13e249eb2_blog.html?utm_term=.c82f6a605475

16 Ray, Michael. "Tea Party movement." Encyclopedia Britannica. https://www.britannica.com/topic/Tea-Party-movement

17 "Believe in America: Mitt Romney's Plan for Jobs and Economic Growth." https://grist.files.wordpress.com/2012/01/believeinamerica-planforjobsandeconomicgrowth-full.pdf

18 Note: The Trump-Pence website does not show the "Make America Great Again" platform that served as the foundation for the 2016 presidential campaign as of this writing. https://www.donaldjtrump.com/

19 Amadeo, Kimberly. "Which President Created the Most Jobs?" The Balance. https://www.thebalance.com/job-creation-by-

president-by-number-and-percent-3863218

20 "Slavery by Another Name." PBS.
    http://www.pbs.org/tpt/slavery-by-another-name/themes/peonage/

21 "Race and Voting in the Segregated South."
    Constitutional Rights Foundation.
    http://www.crf-usa.org/brown-v-board-50th-anniversary/race-and-voting.html

22 "Slavery by Another Name." PBS.
    http://www.pbs.org/tpt/slavery-by-another-name/themes/peonage/

23 Pruitt, Sarah. "5 Myths About Slavery."
    History. http://www.history.com/news/history-lists/5-myths-about-slavery

24 "Communities of Color and the Impacts of
    Sexual Violence." University of Michigan,
    Student Life, Sexual Assault Prevention and
    Awareness Center.
    https://sapac.umich.edu/article/57

25 Christensen, Stephanie. "The Great Migration
    (1915-1960)." Blackpast.org.
    http://www.blackpast.org/aah/great-migration-1915-1960

Chapter 5 – White Supremacy: Psychopathology of Racism

1 Wright, Bobby. "The Psychopathic Racial
   Personality." The Brown Watch.
   http://www.brown-watch.com/what-is-racism/2012/8/31/dr-bobby-wright-the-psychopathic-racial-personality.html

2 *Ibid.*

3   Routledge, Clay. "Exploring the Psychological Motives of Racism." Psychology Today. https://www.psychologytoday.com/blog/more-mortal/201008/exploring-the-psychological-motives-racism

4   Diamond, Stephen A. "How Mad was Hitler?" Psychology Today. https://www.psychologytoday.com/blog/evil-deeds/201412/how-mad-was-hitler

5   Trueman, C.N. "Opposition in Nazi Germany." The History Learning Site. http://www.historylearningsite.co.uk/nazi-germany/opposition-in-nazi-germany/

6   Guaman, Alli. "Afraid of the Red, White and Blue." Study Break. https://studybreaks.com/2017/03/08/american-flag-protest/

7   White, Gillian B. "Revisiting a Jim Crow-Era Guide for Traveling While Black." The Atlantic. https://www.theatlantic.com/business/archive/2016/01/jim-crow-green-book-mlk/424467/

8   Fausset, Richard and Binder, Alan. "Era Ends as South Carolina Lowers Confederate Flag." The New York Times. https://www.nytimes.com/2015/07/11/us/south-carolina-confederate-flag.html?_r=0

9   Obama, Barack. "Transcript: Illinois Senate Candidate Barack Obama." Washingtonpost.com. http://www.washingtonpost.com/wp-dyn/articles/A19751-2004Jul27.html

10 Sheth, Sonam. "The New York Times used 2 full pages to print all of Donald Trump's insults

form the campaign." Business Insider.
http://www.businessinsider.com/new-york-times-prints-donald-trump-campaign-insults-2016-10

11 Lawler, Joseph. "Warren: Trump has more support from KKK than GOP." Washington Examiner.
http://www.washingtonexaminer.com/warren-trump-has-more-support-from-kkk-than-gop/article/2602106

12 Mathis-Lilley. "A Continually Growing List of Violent Incidents at Trump Events." Slate.
http://www.slate.com/blogs/the_slatest/2016/03/02/a_list_of_violent_incidents_at_donald_trump_rallies_and_events.html

13 Abramson, Alana. "How Donald Trump Perpetuated the 'Birther' Movement for Years." ABC News.
http://abcnews.go.com/Politics/donald-trump-perpetuated-birther-movement-years/story?id=42138176

14 "The case of Dred Scott in the United States Supreme Court. The full opinions of Chief Justice Taney and Justice Curtis, and abstracts of the opinions of the other judges; with an analysis of the points rule, and some concluding observahttps://www.loc.gov/resource/llst.020/?st=galleryhttps://www.loc.gov/resource/llst.020/?st=gallerytions." Library of Congress.
https://www.loc.gov/resource/llst.020/?st=gallery

15 Judah, Ben. "Donald Trump's greatest weapon is white Americans' fear that they're quickly

becoming a minority – because they are."
Independent.
http://www.independent.co.uk/voices/donald-trump-us-elections-hillary-clinton-race-hispanic-black-vote-white-americans-fear-minority-a7402296.html

Chapter 6 – Persistence of the American Fiction

1   Noack, Rick. "France 2017: Europe's most decisive election of the year." The Washington Post.
https://www.washingtonpost.com/news/worldviews/wp/2017/05/05/france-2017-europes-most-decisive-election-of-the-year/?utm_term=.5b27e1390c5e

2   Frey, William H. "Diversity defines the millennial generation." The Brookings Institution.
https://www.brookings.edu/blog/the-avenue/2016/06/28/diversity-defines-the-millennial-generation/

Resources

Michelle Alexander, *The New Jim Crow: Mass Incarceration in the Age of Colorblindness* (New York: The New Press, 2010)

American Psychiatric Association: Diagnostic and Statistical Manual of Mental Disorders, Fifth Edition (Arlington: American Psychiatric Association, 2013)

James Baldwin, *The Fire Next Time* (New York: Vintage International, 1993)

Michael Eric Dyson, *Tears We Cannot Stop: A Sermon to White America* (New York: St. Martin's Press, 2017)

Sybrina Fulton and Tracy Martin, *Rest in Power: The Enduring Life of Trayvon Martin* (New York: Spiegel and Grau, 2017)

Eddie Glaude, *Democracy in Black: How Race Still Enslaves the American Soul* (New York: Crown, 2016)

Alison V. Hall, Erika V. Hall, Jamie L. Perry (2016). "Black and Blue: Exploring Racial Bias and Law Enforcement in the Killings of Unarmed Black Male Civilians*," American Psychologist,* The American Psychological Association.

Marc Lamont Hill, *Nobody: Casualties of America's War on the Vulnerable from Ferguson to Flint and Beyond* (New York: Atria, 2016)

Thomas Jefferson, *Notes on the State of Virginia,* annotated edition (New York: Random House, 1997)

Jay Caspian Kang, "How a group of black social-media activists built the nation's first 21st-century civil rights movement," *The New York Times Magazine,* May 10, 2015, p.34

Martin Luther King, Jr., *Where Do We Go From Here: Chaos or Community?* (New York: Harper & Row, 1967)

Shannon Luibrand, "How a death in Ferguson sparked a movement in America," *CBS Interactive News,* August 7, 2015.

Julianne Malveaux, "Black Women Killed by Police by Police are Ignored," *The Dallas Examiner,* May 5, 2015.

Barack Obama, "Remarks by President Obama on the Dallas Police Shooting, July 8, 2016,

David Wall Rice, *Balance: Advancing Identity Theory by Engaging the Black Male Adolescent* (Lanham: Lexington, 2008)

Randall Robinson, *The Debt: What America Owes to Blacks* (New York: Dutton, 2000)

Mychal Denzel Smith, *Invisible Man, Got the Whole World Watching* (New York: Nation Books, 2016)

Brenda Wall, *The Rodney King Rebellion: A Psychopolitical Analysis of Racial Despair and Hope* (Chicago: African American Images, 1992)

Bobby E. Wright, *The Psychopathic Racial Personality and Other Essays* (Chicago: Third World Press, 1985)

ABOUT THE AUTHOR

Dr. Brenda Wall, psychologist, minister and academician, has spent her professional career uplifting and healing the African American community. She has served as vice president at two historically black colleges, as department chair in both graduate and undergraduate psychology programs and has maintained a private clinical practice for over three decades. With degrees from Vassar College, Boston University and George Washington University, she has consistently worked among the people—in their churches, jails, schools, hospitals and neighborhoods. She is the author of **The Rodney King Rebellion** and **The Good Thing about Grief.**

54072231R00092

Made in the USA
San Bernardino, CA
06 October 2017